Mindfulness

How to Relieve Stress, Anxiety and Stress, and Live in Present Happily

(Easy Exercises to Make Mindfulness a Daily Relationship Practice)

Brandon Medeiros

Published by Rob Miles

© **Brandon Medeiros**

All Rights Reserved

Mindfulness: How to Relieve Stress, Anxiety and Stress, and Live in Present Happily (Easy Exercises to Make Mindfulness a Daily Relationship Practice)

ISBN 978-1-989990-81-0

All rights reserved. No part of this guide may be reproduced in any form without permission in writing from the publisher except in the case of brief quotations embodied in critical articles or reviews.

Legal & Disclaimer

The information contained in this book is not designed to replace or take the place of any form of medicine or professional medical advice. The information in this book has been provided for educational and entertainment purposes only.

The information contained in this book has been compiled from sources deemed reliable, and it is accurate to the best of the Author's knowledge; however, the Author cannot guarantee its accuracy and validity and cannot be held liable for any errors or omissions. Changes are periodically made to this book. You must consult your doctor or get professional medical advice before using any of the suggested remedies, techniques, or information in this book.

Upon using the information contained in this book, you agree to hold harmless the Author from and against any damages, costs, and expenses, including any legal fees potentially resulting from the application of any of the information provided by this guide. This disclaimer applies to any damages or injury caused by the use and application, whether directly or indirectly, of any advice or information presented, whether for breach of contract, tort, negligence, personal injury, criminal intent, or under any other cause of action.

You agree to accept all risks of using the information presented inside this book. You need to consult a professional medical practitioner in order to ensure you are both able and healthy enough to participate in this program.

Table of Contents

INTRODUCTION 1

CHAPTER 1: CONCENTRATION 2

CHAPTER 2: MINDFULNESS TO THE RESCUE 21

CHAPTER 3: APPLYING MINDFULNESS IN EVERYDAY LIFE 34

CHAPTER 4: STEP BY STEP INSTRUCTIONS ON HOW TO PERFORM MEDITATION: BEGINNER TECHNIQUES 41

CHAPTER 5: WHAT IS MINDFULNESS? 53

CHAPTER 6: MINDFUL LIVING SURVIVAL GUIDE 64

CHAPTER 7: THE FAMILY CONNECTION 74

CHAPTER 8: MINDFULNESS ON THE BUS OR TRAIN 80

CHAPTER 9: MIND YOUR BREATHING 87

CHAPTER 10: OTHER MINDFULNESS EXERCISES FOR KIDS 93

CHAPTER 11: MINDFULNESS AND INNER AWARENESS .. 100

CHAPTER 12: BENEFITS OF MINDFULNESS MEDITATION 110

CHAPTER 13: WHY PRACTICE MINDFULNESS 121

CHAPTER 14: STREAMLINING YOUR OBLIGATIONS 134

CHAPTER 15: PRACTICING MINDFULNESS IN THE TWENTY-FIRST CENTURY 141

CHAPTER 16: ORIGINS OF MINDFULNESS 149

CHAPTER 17: HOW TO LISTEN MINDFULLY 153

CHAPTER 18: WHO YOU REALLY ARE 160

CHAPTER 19: ADVANCED TIPS FOR RELIEVING WORKPLACE STRESS 173

CHAPTER 20: STRESS AND FLOW STATES 179

CONCLUSION 190

Introduction

The following chapters will discuss some of the many ways our mind can get cluttered. Between work and family stress, it is easy to get bogged down in the day to day grind, leaving little energy left for enjoying the day.

You will discover how important it is to streamline your day to avoid unnecessary mental clutter. Doing so will help you live your best life in a way that is stress-free.

The final chapter will explore some easy ways to maintain a decluttered mind for the long haul.

There are plenty of books on this subject on the market, thanks again for choosing this one! Every effort was made to ensure it is full of as much useful information as possible. Please enjoy!

Chapter 1: Concentration

I want to talk a little bit about goals. When the topic of meditation comes up, people tend to get wishy-washy about goals. It's like the goals of the real world are what they're escaping, so they don't want their meditation practice to have goals. They just want to be able to bliss out and forget the real world. Meditation can offer that temporary relief, but there can be much more than that and goals can help you experience the real rewards of the practice.

First and foremost is regular practice. There is a momentum you build from doing this every day. A lot of people believe that regular practice will actually rewire the brain. I'm not sure if that's an accurate metaphor but you will definitely see results. In the beginning it's important to lay the groundwork and get as much practice in as possible.

Using the noting technique we've taught so far, will provide you with much needed relief from the stresses of everyday life, and more importantly it will give you a break from your narrative-creating brain. This alone, will often propel the practitioner to practice regularly.

You may not experience this benefit immediately. The method of noting may feel a bit clunky at first. It is knacky; you need to get some proficiency at using the labels to note what's happening. In the beginning, this feels like more mental work. Once your mind gets used to this labeling of sensory and mental experience, I promise it will no longer feel like mental work, but a break from the constant flurry of mental activity.

There is a term in meditation used to describe people who get addicted to the good feelings meditation can provide. They are called "jhana junkies." Jhana is a term to describe the levels of relaxation and mental focus one gets while practicing concentration techniques, like the ones described in this book. We are not going to discuss the various signposts that indicate different levels of jhana. They can become a distraction and a wrongheaded goal. I do want to point out that blissing out, while important and actually very useful, should not be the end goal.

For now, creating goals in your meditation practice will keep you focused and help avoid the bliss out trap.

I spent probably a year or so using one meditation technique and just enjoying the bliss-out. It was fun and helped me to build concentration and the ability to relax fairly quickly. I didn't even realize there was anything beyond that technique. So my advice to you is to learn this technique well with the knowledge that this is just the first level of the journey.

In Theravada Buddhist meditation circles, they abandon this first step of building concentration and go straight into what is commonly referred to as "dry Vipassana."

We will deal with this in the next book. What's important about "dry Vipassana" is they go straight for what is called insight or wisdom. They are correct in presupposing that the necessary concentration muscle will be built by going straight into the insight practice. Taking this path is probably better suited for retreats and times when someone can spend countless hours simply practicing the technique. Honestly, it is not too much different than what is taught here; however there are a few slight tweaks that make a huge difference.

I think by slowly building the concentration muscle and incorporating the noting technique into various areas of life, you will create a great foundation for diving into "dry Vipassana" when the time is right. If you dive straight into the insight practice it can be more of a challenge.

I mentioned Shinzen Young earlier. He breaks the art of meditation down into 3 skill areas. After years of practicing these techniques, I have yet to find a better breakdown. Here are the 3 areas you need to build your practice around:

Concentration: This simply refers to the ability to focus your mind on one thing at a time. The two practices we've discussed will help you to do that, both off and on the cushion.

Sensory Clarity: This refers to your ability to parse out the different sensations and thoughts that make up your experience. Remember, everything you experience can only be made up of a combination of one or more of the 5 senses and thinking. There is no experience you have that isn't through the senses. If you can't sense it, you aren't aware of it and therefore aren't experiencing it. As you practice you'll be able to notice more and more subtle sensations.

Equanimity: We haven't really talked about this specifically yet, but this refers to an acceptance of your experience.

Things are happening and you're just being with it. It's not exactly acceptance on a mental level, but more of a lack of resistance. So there might be pain or unpleasant sensations and instead of resisting that, you turn towards it, face it and be with it. With concentration and sensory clarity, this gets easier and easier.

The higher the levels of concentration, sensory clarity and equanimity you have during a meditation or mindfulness session, the more you are progressing. Again, it may be slow going in the beginning, but with just a little bit of practice you'll see ongoing improvement.

There is an interesting theory about concentration that I'll share with you now. I don't know if it's true, but the idea can help motivate your practice sessions. The idea is that our bodies have evolved to give us a reward in the form of good-feeling body sensations when we are fully concentrated on something. Obviously, the more we can concentrate on something the better chance we have at being successful at what we're studying. It is speculated that the ability to concentrate helped with survival and as such, our own bodies reward the practice. It's a pretty cool theory, though difficult to verify. But I've used this as a framework for motivating myself to practice. The better I get at concentration, the better every other aspect of my life will get. Either way, I don't think anyone can argue against developing the ability to concentrate.

I want to talk about a few things the Buddhists call hindrances to the practice. They actually call them the **5 Hindrances**. These are 5 specific problems that may come up during a meditation session and some ideas for dealing with them. Please note that although these problems and solutions are aimed towards meditation practice, I've found that thinking about them during everyday life can also prove to be useful.

Here is a list of the 5 Hindrances, and then we'll talk about each one in detail.

Sensory Desire

Ill Will

Sloth-torpor

Restleness-worry

Doubt

Let's talk about Sensory Desire first. This is a big one. You sit down to meditate or do anything, and you get a feeling that you want to check your phone. Or you want to eat something. Think of this as your body offering up a sensation and your mind wanting to take action on it. It's almost like an emotional itch of desire. This becomes a problem when the desire is to do something or have something other than what you are currently doing or having. This causes internal conflict and suffering.

So what to do about sensory desire? First, use the noting technique on it. Note the body sensations that make it up (feeling, feeling, feeling). Note the thoughts that contribute to it (thinking, thinking, thinking). Remember when I said equanimity is facing things head on and without resistance? This is the perfect time to practice. Although you may still have the desire to check your phone, noting it can often reduce the sensations to a manageable level. You may be surprised at how often the desire just disappears after you have acknowledged it, noted and accepted it. It's almost like the mind is trying to get your attention. "Look at me, don't forget me," the mind shouts and tries to bring up this itch of desire. Remember, at first the mind will not want you to meditate because it is desperately addicted to narrative thinking. Another thing to remember with this is something important in life in general. Have you ever heard the phrase, "You can't get enough of what you don't really need?" If you think about that and apply it to your life, you'll see how true it can be. It's like the excitement of Christmas as a kid and then the emotional hangover after all the presents are opened. All the things you thought you wanted, thought would make you happy, once you get them the happiness only lasts for a little while. Then you're on to the next thing. If you haven't considered this before, consider for a moment that this is true of everything in life. You get a feeling that you want something, you get the thing you want (or drive yourself mad because you don't get the thing you want) and the happiness it brings turns out to be fleeting. Then you're on to the next thing.

I know this is a lofty claim, but meditation can help you to have equanimity to the things you want in life. This is not to say you stop wanting things. Wanting things and getting them is fun, but the actual sensory desire for them is lessened. In this way, you can slow down the rollercoaster of emotions you feel. You still go after goals and have desires; but they don't run your life.

Ok, on to the next of the 5 Hindrances. Ill Will. Otherwise known as Anger. Everyone has felt the rush of anger, the pump of adrenaline shooting through the veins. This can be towards others and towards yourself. Either scenario is not favorable. This could be anger at yourself for being stuck sitting on your cushion for the next hour. It could be anger at your boss for giving you a meaningless job to do. Whatever the situation, leaving anger behind is usually a good idea. Very few well-intentioned plans are devised when angry.

What to do about this one? The answer is so simple you're going to laugh. The answer is to use what the Buddhists call loving-kindness. We will talk more about loving-kindness later on in this book. For now, when you experience Ill Will, let's keep practicing our method of noting it. You could note it feeling, feeling, feeling. I recommend not directly labeling it anger, anger, anger. It always felt like when I used Anger as a label to note, I was fueling the story that these feelings meant Anger. There are times when the blood pressure rises so quickly that you've popped into anger before you even know it, so just noting it using any word is better than not noting. The next time you feel Ill Will towards something, start noting the sensations that make up the experience and see what happens. We'll go into the loving-kindness method later in this book.

Next up on the list is Sloth-torpor. Basically, this refers to laziness and general sleepiness or lethargy. It's exact opposite is the next Hindrance, Restlessness-worry. In this Hindrance, we don't have enough energy. In the next one, we have too much. In a way, they are both the antidote to each other. We are seeking to have energy, but not too much energy. We need balance.

When you are low on energy or mentally dull during meditation, what is one to do? You already know one technique for combatting this. Try Walking Mediation. It typically has a more energizing effect than Sitting Meditation. Do some push-ups. Maybe play a quick game on your phone that requires you to be alert. If you're a coffee drinker, try a small cup (but not too much or you'll have Restlessness-worry as a new problem).

Sometimes, you're just too tired and what you really need is a nap. If you're really that exhausted then by all means go to sleep. Remember, meditation is not meant to torture you. One thing I will recommend though, if you find yourself always being too tired to meditate and taking a nap instead, you're probably running up against mental resistance. It's similar to dealing with pain during meditation. Again, you don't want to torture yourself, but lots of times you will find just pushing through it strengthens your practice.

I used to meditate with a group every Thursday night. Often, I'd be completely beat-up from the week of work and wouldn't feel like meditating. I'd rather go home and watch TV or relax on the couch reading a book with my dog. But I'd force myself to show up and usually within 15 minutes of sitting, I'd feel relaxed and refreshed. By the end of the hour session, I would be completely rejuvenated and alert. So try to push through. It can help you better deal with unpleasant feelings when you need to do something but just don't feel like it.

Restleness-worry is the other side of the coin. This is when you have too much energy. You need to work on calming yourself but you can't sit still. As always, you keep practicing the noting technique to label these sensations and thoughts. If you're too restless for even that and your mind keeps wandering? Try going for a run. Read for some time. Do some stretching or yoga. Note the sensations in your body to try and shift away from your moving mind.

If you drink caffeine on a regular basis, this might be a sign that you need to cut back or switch to decaf. I find that if I drink coffee every day for a couple of months, my mind begins to get restless all the time. When that happens, the first change is to switch to decaf. Although there is a small amount of caffeine in decaf, I find that it replaces the habit of drinking a nice cup of hot coffee in the morning and I don't have the desire for cup after cup to keep the caffeine buzz going. Also, I sleep a lot better when I'm not consuming a lot of caffeine every day. So if this sounds like you, give it a try.

Restlessness during your normal everyday activities can be devastating to your productivity. I would turn off as many notifications on your phone as possible. Try to check email only at certain times so you're not always getting distracted. It's these little things that feed this ongoing restlessness.

Since meditation has a calming effect, if you are restless during the course of the day, 10-15 minutes of practice midday can help steady your mind. That is why I advocate doing a little bit of meditation any time you need to have a clear and alert mind.

Ok, last one and then we finally get on to the fun stuff. The final Hindrance is Doubt. This is originally meant to refer to doubt in the Buddha's teachings. But we're not trying to be Buddhists just better at mindfulness, so we're going to change our definition of this ever so slightly while still retaining the original flavor.

You've gotten this far in the book and I hope you've already started practicing. It takes a certain amount of faith to try something new and go for it. Whenever I try a new practice or technique, I've found it useful to put aside all my notions and preconceptions about what I think is going to happen and just take the training and see what happens. This takes a certain amount of faith in the technique because you don't really know if something works for you until you try it.

Basically, if you are questioning the technique at every step of the way, you'll have a hard time actually trying it out. I am not saying don't question things, absolutely question everything. But you will find if you're questioning things while on the cushion or wondering if things will work while you're practicing, you won't have a lot of good practice sessions.

The mind will want to do this sometimes and it's beyond your control. You're sitting there and the mind yells out that this is stupid. What to do? Note it out. Note the sensations and thoughts that make up the doubt.

Are you starting to see a pattern here? When something comes up, you simply apply the simple technique we've already learned to literally everything. That's why I love this technique so much. No matter what your experience is, the basic instruction holds true - "When in doubt, note it out!"

It also helps to remind yourself from time to time that your ability to concentrate is a worthwhile skill to develop and meditation is a healthy way to unwind and relax. When doubt creeps in at the beginning, you may have to trick yourself a bit to keep going. But with just a little bit of momentum, you will see for yourself how powerful this technique is.

One last note on the 5 Hindrances. What follows is are popular recommendations for dealing with the Hindrances. It's basically an encapsulation about what we've already talked about, using an acronym to make it easy to remember. The acronym is RAIN and here is what it stands for:

Recognize

Accept

Investigate

Non-Identification

Wow, doesn't this sound like what we've already talked about. Recognize sounds an awful lot like acknowledging you are dealing with one of the hindrances. Accept sounds a lot like equanimity. Investigate could be another way of saying "note all the sensory input you are aware of."

Non-Identification is something we're not going to talk about in great detail in this book (but will dive into in the next one). But a phrase commonly used when dealing with anything unpleasant, is "This is not me, this is not mine." You can try it now and see if you get a feeling for what that means, but we will explain exactly the significance of the phrase and precise techniques for having the experience the phrase refers to in later volumes.

See you next chapter.

Chapter 2: Mindfulness To The Rescue

"People have a hard time letting go of their suffering. Out of a fear of the unknown, they prefer suffering that is familiar." - Thích Nhất Hạnh

Do you feel guilty if you relax?

Do you have to win in every game or sport you play?

Do you constantly talk over others or interrupt without meaning to?

Is it normal for you to talk, walk and eat at a rapid pace?

Do you panic when you have spare time at hand?

Do you have trouble quieting your thoughts in order to go to sleep?

Then you are not alone. There are thousands of people like you. Do you feel the need to change? The good news is that if you want to, you can! Through the following chapters we will discuss the different coping strategies one can adopt to overcome these hurdles. However, remember that any suggestion provided in this book will work only if you are ready to make a change. Your determination to succeed is half the battle won. The strategies that are outlined in this book will help you, however, select what steps you would like to take and make a personalized plan consisting of the combination of strategies that will work for you depending on your needs.

The effectiveness of any approach in coping with stress depends upon the circumstances, the individual and the stimuli that is causing the stress.

Coping Strategies

Emotion-focused coping strategy. This involves reducing any negative emotional response related to stress. They can include fear, anxiety, embarrassment, frustration or depression. Emotion–based coping can reduce the feeling of distress caused by the stress. This is especially helpful when the cause of stress is outside of your control. An example of this would be the delay in a flight's departure – this is clearly beyond your control so worrying about it will not change the outcome. In cases like these, you may:

1) **Shift focus to other matters**. When you accept that there is something causing you stress, consciously put it on the back burner until you are in a calmer frame of mind to deal with it.

2) **Let off steam in a healthy way**. Release pent up emotions by venting with a trusted confidante or even journaling. This reduces the likelihood that the suppressed emotions will eventually explode with undesirable results.

In extreme cases, drug therapy prescribed by a physician may be required. This is because the drug focuses on the emotion aroused and hence it can be very effective. However, this is not meant to be used frequently or as a long term treatment.

Problem-focused coping strategy. These techniques deal directly with the problem that is causing the stress and works on tackling the issue head-on to reduce the impact on the individual. Problem-focused coping is most effective if the stress can be managed by changing the situation. This method may include:

1) **Take control**. This involves changing the relationship between you and the stress. Instead of allowing the stress control your emotions, you control it or totally incapacitate it. For example, an entrepreneur with a small landscaping company may love going out on-site and working with clients on their dream gardens but be thoroughly intimidated by the necessary tasks of scheduling sub-contractors and billing clients. By hiring an assistant, he can avoid the stress of dealing directly with the tasks that he finds stressful.

2) **Seek Information**. This is a rational approach to the problem which will certainly appeal to the strategizer in the Type A individual. Let's say, for example,

the unavailability of airline tickets becomes a source of stress - you can do some research to find other options whether by changing airlines, flight times or some other variable. By shifting the focus from the cause of the stress to the more active role of getting information on how to solve the problem, you will get immediate relief from the anxiety.

3) **Assess pros and cons**. Analyze the situation and weigh the pros and cons associated with different courses of action. Discussing it with someone else can provide another perspective to help with the decision-making.

In many cases, problem-focused coping strategies yields quicker and more lasting results as they address the root cause of the stress. These are also typically in the wheelhouse of the Type A individual who prefers action to the more phlegmatic approach of the emotional-based strategies. Nevertheless, in some situations, a problem-focused strategy will not work. For serious health issues, for example, you cannot apply a problem-focused approach as the situation cannot be 'solved' using problem-solving techniques.

While both types of strategies will work in different scenarios, and are certainly good tools to keep in the toolbox, this book seeks to suggest another strategy which can be a game-changer for the individual who struggles with some of the more difficult Type A tendencies. These behavior patterns are not merely fodder for water-cooler jokes and friendly office jabs, they can be a source of acute embarrassment and the cause of alienation for millions of individuals who, despite their best efforts, stick out like a sore thumb amongst co-workers, classmates, friends and even family. Mindfulness brings equanimity to the Type A soul. It trains the mind to be fully present at every moment, experiencing every thought and impulse but anchored in a stillness and reacting only through that filter.

Why Mindfulness?

In recent times, scientific research has proven that the positive effects of meditation reach down to our cells and strengthen the body from within. In the 2009 Nobel Prize-winning study by Dr. Elizabeth Blackburn (co-authored with Carol W. Greider and Jack W. Szostak), 'Can meditation slow rate of cellular aging? Cognitive stress, mindfulness and telomeres', she expounded on the harmful effects of psychological stress on physiology. She found that psychological stress and its intimate partner violence may accelerate cellular aging thus shortening lifespan. In other words, using the technique of mindfulness, one can reduce stress, which reduces the flow of excess hormones in the body which in turn reduces damage to the cellular structure thereby promoting good health and longevity.

Centuries ago, life was extremely different from life as we know it today. Early humans lived a very simple life. They were hunter-gatherers whose lives revolved around finding food, shelter and protection from wild animals and other humans. There was no agriculture, no buildings, and no civilization. The present-day man has virtually the same genetic makeup, not much has changed. However, we have transformed our environment to an incredible degree. Let us consider the 'fight or flight' response which was used in the past when the need arose to escape from physical harm or danger. In modern times, our complex and fast-paced lifestyle requires us to use this 'fight or flight' response very often. The same stress-induced response that was used by our primitive ancestors is the same response that we have whether we are late for an appointment, suddenly pulled over by the police, or arrive at an exam for which we are unprepared. Our physiological makeup, designed for the slower-paced, simpler life of earlier times is ill-suited to handle this type of stress on a regular basis. Sadly, this is the reason the more driven, emotional and 'stress-prone' Type A individual is more likely to have a mental breakdown or heart attack because his or her response is so much more intense than say the more laid-back demeanor of someone with Type B tendencies.

Many therapists recommend mindfulness as an effective tool to ease problems related to anxiety. It is the non-judgmental, accepting and intentional focus on one's emotions, sensations and thoughts that go along with them. The tremendous success of mindfulness has made it popular worldwide as the basis for cognitive and behavioral therapy programs.

Mindfulness meditation is considered to be at the heart of ancient Buddhist traditions. In the west, mindfulness-based stress reduction techniques were popularized by Jon Kabat Zinn. Long believed to promote well-being, mindfulness has been accepted as an aspect of consciousness. Since the 1970's, clinical psychologists have employed mindfulness-based therapy to treat various psychological conditions using ancient healing techniques. The mental and physical health benefits of these programs have been clinically documented and the success of mindfulness-based stress relief is widely acknowledged.

To check the efficacy of this therapy, studies were sponsored by The National Institutes of Health's National Center for Complementary and Alternative Medicine. The results showed that it helped most of the participants improve their self-esteem and their use of pain-relieving drugs reduced significantly. Various models of mindfulness-based programs have since been adopted in different settings such as schools, hospitals, veteran-centers and correctional facilities.

Apart from non-meditative exercises, mindfulness also involves formal and informal meditation. It is a successful blend of body-awareness, yoga and meditation so that the virtues of all three can be experienced together. Through this, a person learns the skills to be able to cope with the challenges of everyday life, stress and pain. One also learns to gracefully handle disturbing episodes in life and to live in the moment. Mindfulness has multiple benefits as it deals with all aspects of mind and body.

Mindfulness is about being fully alive and awake within yourself. This experience is always available within us, but we often lose sight of it when we go through any period of depression or trauma caused by internal or external pressure. The mind is a common factor in stress and other related disorders, so engaging its power to bring about a positive change is an intuitive response. I would suggest that it is because of this holistic approach that it has the potential of yielding such enduring benefits for the Type A individual.

The capacity for learning, healing, transformation and growth are all within us. This method of meditation teaches us to tap into these inner resources. Mindfulness meditation teaches us to attain contentment in and derived from the present moment and to achieve a sense of completeness just from being. In this relaxed state of awareness, we observe the outer world with its constant changes without attempting to control any aspect of it. We also observe our inner world of sensations, emotions and thoughts without judgment or recrimination.

These incredible qualities make mindfulness a perfect fit for the a Type A personality. The practice can benefit people from all races and religions. It represents the happy union of the knowledge gained from years of scientific research and centuries-old Buddhist meditative traditions and it has the power to revolutionize your life.

Chapter 3: Applying Mindfulness In Everyday Life

The best way to make mindfulness a part of your daily life is to develop a genuine love for it. When you find a deep connection with the practice of mindfulness, and when you make it a part of your personal identity, it becomes effortless to put it into practice consistently.

How do you apply mindfulness in daily life? What are the steps to take in order to not just let meditation be a momentary spark of interest for you?

Here are some ways for you to incorporate mindfulness into your life:

Enjoy the Pleasure of Being Alone

There are times when you love the company of others, but simply spending some time with yourself can also replenish your energy in several ways. During moments when you are alone, allow yourself to become mindful of the present moment. Let thoughts of the past and future drift away and focus on whatever it is in front of you.

For instance, if you are alone in your bedroom, bring your awareness towards your surroundings. Pay attention to the shapes and colors that are right in front of your eyes, the personality of the scent in your room, or the feel of the fabric of your bed against your skin. Listen to the sounds inside your room, be it the hum of your fan, the stillness of silence, or the chirping of birds right outside your window.

Action Plan: Set aside even just 10 minutes of each day to be alone. Try to make it the same time every day, such as between 7:00 to 7:10 in the morning, find a time that works for you. Spend that time focusing on just the present moment, what you are experiencing right then in the moment. Do not plan for what is coming up in the future or write the things that transpired in your journal. Focus on the present moment as it truly is and let all thought drift away, instead.

Spend Time in Nature

Whether you believe in the spiritual or not, you will find an instant connection to something deeper within you when you spend some time in nature. It is much easier to be mindful when you are surrounded by natural things, whether it is at a park full of old trees in the middle of the city, or in a small garden with freshly cut grass in your backyard.

Observe how nature continues to grow despite your efforts to create unnatural things. Like a tree's roots that weave through cracks in a pavement, nature manages to be constant and persistent. The best part is that nature is beauty in and of itself. There is no need to groom or maintain it for it to capture your senses. All you have to do is let it be to enjoy it. By spending some time with nature, you can reconnect with your own true self.

Action Plan: Once a week, connect with nature in one way or another. Whenever you can, take a trip to the beach or a natural park and take a walk. During the busiest weeks, go to a nearby garden to just appreciate the blooms and growing plants. Literally stop and smell the flowers. Spend some quiet time looking up at the sky to observe the clouds or the stars. Give it a try and you will soon realize how much more meaningful life can be.

Practice Being Grateful Each Day

Expressing thankfulness and appreciation for everything good, which is going on in your life is the easiest way to cultivate positive thoughts. By being grateful, you also get to know some aspects of your life you may have taken for granted. Gratitude plays a major role in mindfulness meditation, because when you meditate, you don't only focus on the present moment. You are also doing it with an open and grateful attitude.

Action Plan: There are several ways for you to express gratitude for the little things. The easiest would be to say thank you to anyone who has helped you, no matter how small the gesture. When you recognize someone else's efforts to be generous, you will notice that you also feel freer and more alive.

Another is to end each day with a reflection on the events and people you are grateful for. Even just for a minute, think about three things that made you feel good about that day.

For instance, you can say, "I am thankful for the hot coffee that I got to enjoy this morning. It helped me gain the energy to finish my morning task. I am grateful for the rain today, because it made the atmosphere cooler and cozier as I worked in my office. I am thankful for my mother, who lovingly prepared a roast beef sandwich for me so that I could enjoy a delicious lunch."

Let Go

Everyone has gone through hardships in their life. Some may consider theirs much worse than others, but everything boils down to the fact that life constantly presents change. Nothing in life is permanent, after all. However, what makes it difficult for some is that they become too attached to certain things, events and people. This causes them to suffer when a change occurs.

Through mindfulness, you can learn how to let go of these attachments. It may be hard at first, but eventually, the pain will subside. What mindfulness does is it teaches you to acknowledge your own attachments. By accepting it, you can move towards letting them go.

Action Plan: Whenever you are upset about something, reflect on the qualities that make it challenging for you to let it go. This may be a difficult thing to do, especially if you have gone through a loss, such as a breakup or a passing of a loved one. It can also be difficult to let go of negative thoughts, especially if someone did you wrong in the past.

However, by reflecting on it, you are also acknowledging your attachment to it. When you do, you will find that it is no longer a part of your present moment. The present moment is your true reality, not the thought of the thing, which makes you feel angry or sad. By recognizing this fact, it will be easier for you to let go more easily.

For instance, forgiving someone for his or her transgression towards you in the past is one way of letting go. Likewise, expressing gratitude towards the time you had spent with a departed loved one will help you move on as well. By letting go and focusing on the present moment, you also free yourself from the suffering caused by attachment.

Making mindfulness a part of your everyday life will help you appreciate each moment. Moreover, it lets you make wiser decisions that can lead you to a better path and more fruitful opportunities. Best of all, you will become free from regret and rumination. Once you have reached the end of your life, you can then look back on it with a kind, open and grateful heart.

Chapter 4: Step By Step Instructions On How To Perform Meditation: Beginner Techniques

There are many people who know quite a few meditation exercises, but they don't really practice them. The reason being it is difficult for them to sit still for even a few minutes, let alone ten, fifteen, or twenty minutes.

 May be your knees or back start hurting, and you think you might do your body some irreparable damage. Or your body gets itchy in the most uncommon places and you just can't help scratching. Or every odd sound starts catching your attention.

Elements of Meditation

The different forms of meditation may employ different techniques but they share the following same elements:

Focused attention

Concentrated attention is the most vital component of meditation. When you focus your attention, you are able to set your mind free from day-to-day distractions that often cause tension and anxiety, and venture into a world of calmness, clarity and peace. What you focus on will vary depending on the type of meditation you are doing.

Peaceful breathing

To achieve relaxed, deep, even-paced breathing, it is important that you breathe using your diagram. Using your diaphragm is more efficient because it requires minimal action from your shoulders and neck muscles. The objective of slow and deep breathing is to bring more oxygen into your body. This calms you and creates an inner space that is conducive to meditation.

Quiet and comfortable setting

Advanced practitioners can perform meditation almost anywhere, even if the place is noisy or crowded. As a beginner, it is advisable for you to start practicing meditation in a quiet and comfortable place where you won't be distracted by others.

Before you start your meditation practice, get rid of any distractions. Turn off the television, radio and cell phone before you begin each session.

Sitting Up Straight

Fortunately, a few well-implemented meditation poses can give your body amazing results and make the experience a lot more enjoyable for you. Regardless of the sitting posture you opt for, you'll be able to enjoy it even more if you have a flexible and strong lower back. After all, you'll get the required support from your body. As you stretch your hips to sit in a cross-legged position, you'll discover that you can sit without putting any additional pressure on your knees.

Once you've selected the postures that work best for you, make sure to practice them carefully and gently. Treat your bod kindly and respectfully. Experience the stretch, but retreat gently in case it gives you any pain.

Another important thing to remember is to use a rug or meditation mat between your sensitive body parts and the flooring.

Cobra Pose

Termed for its close resemblance to the elegant serpent, this posture provides your back and spine with an amazing backward stretch. What's more, this pose prevents you from slouching forward. Use only your upper back to begin this stretch, and then slowly spread it down your back.

Follow these steps to practice this posture.

Lie such that your forehead rests on the floor.

Set your hands below your shoulders. Your fingertips should face forward. Also, the external edge of your hands should be even with those of your shoulders.

Pull your elbows in such that your arms get in touch with your torso's sides.

Maintain your feet close to each other. Press your thighs and legs into the floor.

Move your chest gradually away from the floor. While keeping your neck and head aligned with your spine, lift and extend from the upper back.

Relax your shoulders. Press the chest forward and upward gently. Open the abdomen while you push your pubic bone into the ground.

Take smooth and deep breaths.

Maintain the pose for at least five full breaths.

Gradually unfold the posture as you breathe out.

As you once again lie down with the forehead rested on the floor, relax completely.

Cat Pose

Have you ever seen a cat stretching itself after taking a nap? This posture has got its name from there.

This posture not only helps you stretch and support your spine and back for the sitting position, but it also enables you to give your day a fresh start. As soon as you get out of your comfy bed in the morning, sit in the Cat posture for about ten to twenty minutes of meditation practice, and then you're good to go.

Follow these steps to practice the Cat posture:

Get on your knees and hands. Keep the spine horizontal. Make sure your thighs and arms are at 90-degree to the floor.

With every breath you exhale, flex the spine upward like a cat. Stretch your body at the tailbone.

As the stretch is about to culminate, tuck the chin a little.

With every breath you inhale, flex the spine downward. Start with the tailbone and lift your head a bit as the stretch ends.

Continue stretching and breathing in this manner for about ten or twenty minutes.

Cradle Stretch

Helping you open and stretch your hips, this particular posture is all about holding your leg in the arms. Make sure to lift the leg gently and gradually.

Follow the given steps to practice this posture.

Sit straight on the floor such that your legs are spread in the front.

Flex one knee. Let your thigh be rotated to the side. Hold the lower leg in both your arms. Clasp your hands. Use the fold of one elbow to hold the knee and the fold of the other knee to hold your foot.

Keep the head straight and spine in the extended position. Rock the leg gently from one side to another.

Maintain the rocking position for at least five breaths. Inhale deep and smooth breaths.

Slowly put the leg down and repeat the same steps for the other leg.

Locust Pose

This posture resembles a grasshopper when its abdomen is suspended into the air. Since it stretches and supports your lower back, this posture provides you with the strength you need to sit up straight.

If you're an amateur meditator, start with the half Locust posture and then proceed to the full Locust pose whenever you think your lower back is strong enough. Make slow and smooth progress. Avoid any painful movements.

Follow these steps to practice this posture. Lie down such that your chin rests on the floor. Place your arms at the sides. Keep your palms up.

With both hands, make a partial fist. Adjust your arms below your body. Set your hands below your pubic bone such that your thumbs touch lightly.

Now you can practice either the full locust or half locust according to your ease.

Full Locust – Inhale and contract the muscles of your buttock a bit. As you breathe out, lift both your legs into the air, but don't bend your knees. Maintain the posture for at least five breaths. Inhale deeply and smoothly into your abdomen. Lower both your legs. Turn the head to any side and calm down.

Half Locust – Inhale and contract the muscles of your buttock a bit. As you breathe out, lift any one leg into the air, but don't bend your knee. Maintain the posture for at least five breaths. Lower the leg and repeat the same steps for the second leg. Repeat multiples times on every side. Turn the head to any side and calm down.

Enjoying the book so far? Leave a review!

Butterfly Pose

This posture proves to be a great challenge for athletes as well as a runner. It stretches and gives amazing support to the groin, hip, and inner thigh.

Follow the given steps to practice this posture.

Sit straight on the floor such that both your legs are stretched in the front.

Flex your knees. Bring your feet soles along with the external edges of your feet on the floor.

Clasp the hands together and then grasp your feet. Pull the heels of your feet in in the direction of your groin. Push the knees in the direction of the floor while you extend your spine.

Maintain the posture for at least five breaths. Make sure to inhale smooth and deep breaths into the abdomen.

While breathing out, let go of your feet. Spread your legs in the front and calm down.

Lunge Pose

Usually considered a back stretch, this posture supports and stretches your hips. If you don't have much time to try too many postures, just combine the Lunge posture with Cat posture to develop your own mini routine.

Follow the given steps to practice this posture.

Get on your knees and hands. Keep the spine horizontal. Make sure your thighs and arms are at 90-degree to the floor.

Take your left knee a bit forward. While keeping the heel of your left leg close to the right side of your groin, set it on the floor.

Spread the right leg behind you. Keep it straight. Make sure your knee faces downward.

Place your pubic bone such that it points toward the floor. Lift the chest forward and upward. Put your weight on the right leg and arms.

Maintain the posture for at least five breaths.

Repeat the same steps for the other side.

Chapter 5: What Is Mindfulness?

Understanding the meaning of mindfulness before you can start applying it to improve your life is of vital importance. Simply put, mindfulness is a state of being present and fully aware of your present self.

It means focusing your attention on what is happening in your mind and body. It involves paying attention to your bodily sensations, your feelings, your thoughts, the emotions you are experiencing, and what you are doing now.

Mindfulness also means being fully aware of everything happening within you without being critical or judgmental about it. It involves paying attention to what is going on without thinking about the good and bad side of it.

It involves fully accepting the presumed good and bad within you and being compassionate and at peace with it. When situations related with negativity occur, you simply observe them and let them pass, choosing not to take them personally. This helps you gain control of your life.

When you put your life on autopilot, your mind always drifts from moment to moment, from place to place, from emotion to emotion. You constantly shift your focus to the past, anticipate events of the future, but fail to appreciate what happens now.

You fail to listen to the signals your body is giving you and torture yourself with self-criticism. Over time, you lose your self-control, your emotional stability, and self-appreciation. You become moody, stressed, depressed, anxious, angry, and you generally feel miserable.

The truth is that mindfulness is in all of us. It is innate and inborn. When you drift away from the present and what is happening to you right now, a certain unseen force will try to bring you back to it. That is mindfulness. However, to be mindful and make the most out of it, with the goal being to achieve the fulfilling life you have always wanted, you need to put in effort and practice. That is what this book will focus on providing you with: a way back to being mindful, but before that, we will look at the history of mindfulness.

Mindfulness: A Brief History

Mindfulness has its roots in the traditions of Buddhism. A man who discovered its effectiveness through curiosity incorporated into Buddhist teachings. His name was Siddhārtha Gautama.

Back then, Mindfulness became a key Buddhist tradition because it provided the believer with wisdom. The practice in itself involved meditation. The person would sit with legs crossed and eyes closed and focus on the breath as it flowed in and out of his body. If the person's thoughts started drifting, in a non-judgmental manner, the person was to return to focusing only on breathing.

In the 1980s, a man called John Kabat-Zinn, a mental health student, introduced this practice to the western population. Mindfulness as a powerful technique that improved mental well-being fascinated Kabat-Zinn. He set out to research it at the Stress Reduction Clinic in Umass Medical School (later renamed to Center for Mindfulness Research and Practice).

He studied this technique with an aim of testing how effective it was on restlessness, cognition, and emotion and documented it in a program he called Mindfulness-Based Stress Reduction (MBSR).

Later, mindfulness became part of clinical psychology and psychiatry after MBSR results showed its effectiveness at regulating emotion. Since then, many experts started adopting mindfulness as a strategy to provide clients with techniques that improve their physical and mental conditions like reducing symptoms of stress, depression, and worry.

Today, psychiatrists and psychologists effectively use mindfulness to help those suffering from mental illness and disorders, stress, anxiety, and even drug addiction. Furthermore, many studies published based on MBSR, document the health benefits of this technique. Because of this, mindfulness has gained worldwide popularity and attention in many places like in schools, hospitals, and prisons.

Facts About Mindfulness

There are a few facts about mindfulness that as a beginner you should know about and become aware of them. They are:

Mindfulness is not a form of religion; it is simply a way of training your mind. Mindfulness involves meditation, an act commonly perceived as religious. To practice mindfulness, you do not have to change your religious beliefs or otherwise. Anyone can practice mindfulness.

To practice mindfulness meditation, you do not have to sit down and cross your legs. You may have seen this in films or magazines, but the truth is that it is not a requirement. Meditation is something you or anyone can do anywhere and at any position you choose to be in. You can do it while seated in a chair, travelling on a bus, or even when walking. Nevertheless, if you want to, you can meditate seated with your legs crossed in the lotus or half lotus poses.

Mindfulness is not a time consuming task. Many people make up excuses for why they cannot meditate because they feel it takes too much time. The truth is that while mindfulness does need a lot of patience and persistence, it barely takes more time than that which you can afford to lose. Mindful meditation takes roughly five to ten minutes. Furthermore, the results are worth the time and effort. You will find that after this exercise, you will be relaxed and this will enable you to get things done faster.

Mindfulness is not a practice based on the faith you have in it. As a technique, mindfulness draws on collected evidence and is a practice recommended after scientific experiments and research determined its helpfulness and effectiveness. Therefore, mindfulness is a proven technique backed by research and experience that proves it has positive results on your health, mood, work relationships, and other important areas of your life.

Mindfulness is not a practice that attempts to deter your mind from focusing on the valuable things you hope to achieve in life, nor is it there to change your belief and perspective of things in your life. Instead, mindfulness helps you view things with greater clarity. With this clarity, you make wiser judgments about events and circumstances, and find the optimum path to achieving your goals as well as that which you truly desire in life.

Mindfulness is not a special or a new complicated thing. It is something you are already familiar with. Deep inside you, you have the capacity to be in the present moment. All it takes to be mindful is a few simple practices that will help you cultivate the innate ability you have and use it to improve yourself.

Let us now look at how important mindfulness is.

Importance Of Mindfulness

Mindfulness is a powerful practice whose numerous benefits are more than you could ever imagine. Here are some of them:

1: It Helps Lower Stress Levels

One reason why you may lose your self-control and become emotionally unstable is increased levels of stress in your body. For most people, we are always stressed because we don't learn to live in the moment but worry about the future and regret about our past mistakes.

When you practice mindfulness, you place yourself in a position to learn how to focus on the present. This reduces the crowd of thoughts that causes stress. The result of this is that you feel relaxed, calm, and able to manage stress effectively.

2: Helps Guard Against Mental Illness

Mindfulness, if practiced frequently, can help you prevent incidences of mental disorders like depression and anxiety. Research by mental health professionals at the University of Oregon has proven that mindful meditation can help stimulate important connections in the brain called axonal density and increase certain protective tissues of the brain called myelin tissue.

The formation of this network of signal and increase in the protective tissue ensures general good health in your brain and helps prevent mental illnesses and other disorders.

3: Helps Reduce Feelings of Loneliness in Elderly People

Loneliness in elderly people can be particularly dangerous and can cause emotional instability, lack of self-esteem, and several health risks like depression.

Practicing mindfulness can help eliminate this.

Research suggests that mindfulness helps you focus on the present. In the end, this practice helps eliminate other negative emotions like anger and loneliness, emotions that can become detrimental to your health.

4: Helps Improve Weight Loss

When stressed, you will want to do anything to feel better. Most people turn to comfort food high in sugar and calories to feel better. This will definitely lead to weight gain.

Mindfulness helps you control your stress. This causes you to become more aware of what you do, and what happens around you, including your eating habits and patterns. This helps you avoid and lose excess weight.

5: Helps Improve Sleep

With the busy days we face at work and the unfinished projects we constantly try to keep up with, it becomes generally difficult to switch off these stressing thoughts. These disturbances keep us from getting adequate sleep.

Mindful meditation helps you focus on the present and the task you are working on. This includes focusing on sleep when it is time to sleep. The more you practice mindfulness, the more you learn how to focus easily and have adequate sleep.

Chapter 6: Mindful Living Survival Guide

There are many challenges that are present in mindful living and these are the reasons why people find it hard to stay committed. The road to mindful living is all about taking one step at a time. This chapter will give you tips on how to do mindful living despite of all the obstacles around you.

With the many distractions that we face each day, it is no wonder why it is easy for people to get lost in everything. There are many roadblocks in achieving mindful living. In order for you to do mindful living, it is crucial that you take care of all facets of your life. Below is your survival guide to make mindful living a way of life.

Physical Healing

Mindful healing is not always associated with physical healing but it works wonders in helping people heal from their suffering. It is a good way for us to reconnect to our bodies and appreciate ourselves, love our capabilities and embrace our limitations. Below are the ways on how you can apply mindfulness in physical healing.

Listen To Your Body

It is important that you listen to your body at all times. To do mindfulness of the body, it is important that you meditate before going to bed because it is an extremely relaxing thing that leads to deep sleep. Mindfulness to the body can bring relief and reduce the feeling of pains and aches. It is also a great way to dispel stress. But more importantly, mindfulness of the body allows you to listen closely to what your body is telling you so that you can detect signs that your body is okay or not.

Do Compassion Meditation

This is generally done by focusing your attention on other people. You do compassion meditation by thinking of people whom you love. Think of your loved ones (mother, father, wife, husband, son or daughter) and once that you have that person in your mind, focus only on feelings of love as well as appreciation for that individual.

Emotional Healing

Emotional healing is as important as physical healing. Mindful living is a good therapy for people who are suffering from emotional turmoil. Below are practices that you can do to promote healing of your emotions through mindful living.

Forgiveness Meditation

Anger and all other negative emotions can consume everything positive within us thus making them difficult to overcome. However, one practice of mindfulness that you can use to promote emotional healing is forgiveness meditation. Forgiveness meditation is basically focusing on how you have harmed yourself, how you have harmed others and how others have harmed you. You need to reflect on your pain and let the feelings stay within you so that you can process the entire situation before letting it go and forgiving yourself and other people as well as asking other people for forgiveness. As soon as you let go and forgive, try to be aware of the feelings and thoughts that are attached to the whole process of forgiveness and being forgiven.

Going Home

This refers to a mindfulness breathing exercise which is good for mental as well as emotional healing. It allows us to diver peace within the moment so that we can finally let go of the things that are holding us back. To do this breathing exercise, you need to stop what you are doing, breathe deeply and follow your breathing to achieve mindfulness and peace.

Cultivating Nourishing Relationship

Another important aspect in mindful living is the relationship. The problem is that relationships can be very tricky and it requires constant communication to keep all channels open. However, how can you keep an open channel of relationship if you are so busy doing other things? Below are the things that you need to do to cultivate nourishing relationship through mindful living.

Mindful Speech

Mindful speech is all about being aware of the words that you are speaking and also knowing the effect of your words to a person at a given moment. This is all about understanding the power of words that we utter. Words are very important as it can build relationships or severe them. To practice mindful speech, you are aware of the message that you are communicating to other people and you are also aware of the effects that they can have to others. So if you want to nourish relationships, then use the right words.

Mindful Listening

Mindful listening is all about being aware of the conversation and really listening to the person with all your being. By focusing your undivided attention to other people, you will be able to listen more than the words that they say. Listening mindfully also prevents you from making quick judgment based on the conversation that you just heard.

Dealing with Craving

Craving can difficult to control but mindful living does not only help us manage our addiction but it can also be used to discover the source as well as treat your addiction so that it will be gone for good. Below are tips on how to deal with craving using mindful living.

Mindful Indulging

Mindful indulging is a form of meditation which cuts the root of your addiction or craving. When you crave for something, you need to partake on the craving while being mindfully present during the entire experience. Pay attention to your thoughts and feelings while partaking in your craving. By paying close attention to your feelings, you might discover that being mentally connected to your craving can damage your life and relationship with other people so you can now exert effort in controlling your cravings.

Tree Of Life Meditation

Mindful indulging is a great way to cut the root of your craving but the Tree of Life meditation is a practice that allows you to gain control when your craving intensifies. This is a meditation practice done while sitting in a lotus position. Shift your attention to your abdomen and feel the strength of your abdomen and imagine that it is a trunk of a big tree that is firmly rooted on the ground. Breathe until you release all your anxieties and cravings away from your body.

Finding Mindfulness despite Mayhem

People tend to believe that mindful living requires one to live in an almost monk-like existence. They think that people who are able to achieve mindfulness do nothing but drink green tea, do yoga and read spiritual texts. In reality, not everyone is blessed with living such as passive and relaxing life. The thing is that people can still do mindful living even in the midst of mayhem. This means that they can still be one with their thoughts and inner self even if they are walking in the middle of a highly trafficked city street. This section will discuss how you can find mindfulness despite the mayhem and chaos around you.

Do Unit Tasking

Don't make your life more complicated as it is by doing multitasking. What you need is to do unit tasking and make sure that each task that you do is your entire universe. Take one task at a time and do it mindfully as possible. Stay with the task until it is completed. Remember that life is not a big to-do list so enjoy life by doing one thing at a time.

Use Mindfulness Bells

In some remote areas, the church bell rings each day and once people hear the bell ringing, they stop with whatever it is that they are doing and take the moment as it is. The small pauses that we do each day allows us to connect deeply with ourselves and with life in the present. You can use a mindfulness bell to remind you to stop and meditate at regular intervals within the day. You can set the alarm clock in your smart phone to help you keep track of your meditation "schedule".

Devise Mini Meditations throughout the Day

While meditating for a long time is very important in achieving mindfulness, taking mini meditations throughout the day can help you get by even if mayhem is staring at your face. Mini meditations can take only for a minute and what you can do is that if you feel burned out or stressed, you need to stop with whatever it is you are doing to meditate and clear your minds and emotions from all the things that are bothering you. In fact, taking a minute of mindfulness several times each day can make you more effective compared to not taking a break at all. So take your breaks wisely and use it for meditation. A minute of meditation can do wonders for your mental and physical health so that you can face all obstacles in your life feeling positive and grateful.

Chapter 7: The Family Connection

We are all born into a family, but we are also part of the family of the human race. There may be people in your life who are not that close anymore or who you can't really relate to. People think on different planes, but the way that you open your heart to all of mankind pays you back immensely. Thus, if you selfishly stay in your own cocoon, you lose the opportunity to spread a little light into the lives of others. We briefly touched upon this in Chapter 2 but there's much more to the connection you feel with others than simply smiling.

Let's look at what you can do to help you to feel that you are increasing your worth and also increasing the happiness of others.

Keep in touch

While you may feel that you have very little in common with the parents who brought you into the world, you actually have a lot to feel grateful for because of their contribution to your life. That doesn't mean you owe them a debt as such, but it does mean that appreciation goes a long way toward having a peaceful heart. Even in a dysfunctional family, people need to feel loved.

Pick up the phone and let your parents know your latest news, but don't make the call all about you. Let your parents tell you about their news and listen attentively because these are people who are older and who perhaps don't have as much contact with you as they wish they had. The problem is that too many people hold grudges against parents and, at the end of the day, holding grudges makes you suffer more than it makes them suffer. Let go. Until you do, you will never feel the freedom that you are entitled to.

Offer your service

If you live near to one of your siblings and you haven't really kept in touch much, now's the time to bridge the gap. Visiting and taking something nice with you isn't that hard. What you are doing is opening up avenues for yourself to sense that joy that comes from giving. Even if you just pass by with a cake from the bakery, it's a nice gesture and gives you a five minute break from your routine that you can share in the company of someone else. Be mindful of what your sibling is saying and help to make your sibling feel you are really interested in what he/she has to say.

Break the generation gap

Sometimes we leave people behind in our lives because they are old and don't really think in the same way as we do, but visiting grandparents can be something rewarding for both of you because your grandparents have lived very long lives and may just be able to help you in ways that you don't yet appreciate. For example, in recounting their stories, sometimes you pick up gems of wisdom that you would never have asked advice on, but nonetheless are valuable to you.

Bear in mind that old people lived in a time when people cared more. Bake a cake to show you care and even if it isn't perfect, your grandparents will enjoy it.

Mindful evening meal

Sometimes your kids can't be there for the evening meal, so don't make a huge fuss because this alienates kids even more. Instead of doing that, make a point of making the evening meal that you do have together something memorable.

Teach the kids about mindful eating. This means taking time to eat the food on their plates. It means trying to experience all of the textures of the foods and describing them. It means enjoying the freshness of the food and celebrating the aroma. If you try this with kids from an early age, they will appreciate all of those tastes in the future and are less likely to opt for bad choices. You can also use mindful eating yourself to lessen the potential of illness. Much of the time these days, we eat on the go which contributes so much to digestive problems and illnesses.

Bedtime and storytime

When it comes to the evening, most parents are glad to get the little monsters off to bed. When you are mindful in your life, you begin to realize that each night when your children go to bed, it's one less day ahead of them in their childhood, one less day to enjoy and remember.

You need to be there in that moment. Try taking your guitar up with you and singing a song together or a favorite book and reading it together, playing the part of the characters in the book and making them come to life in the child's eyes. Being mindful includes moments that you may otherwise take for granted. This is an opportunity to shine. Finish off the evening ritual with a prayer of thanks, even if it is not anything to do with religion. Hold hands with your kids in a circle and thank life for giving you all the chance to share such wonderful times together.

Being mindful with your family helps to bring them up to be mindful too. That also helps them to live life to its best and to be able to appreciate the life they are given.

Chapter 8: Mindfulness On The Bus Or Train

If you utilize public transportation you can take the time spent getting where you are going to practice mindfulness meditation as effectively as if you were sequestered peacefully in your own home. There is one caveat however, in order to practice mindfulness meditation effectively it is important that you feel comfortable in the space in which you find yourself. If you find yourself in a situation where something requires your full attention you will likely be unable to reach your full mindfulness meditation potential.

While listening to music while practicing mindfulness meditation in public is not recommended, you may find it helpful to wear headphones as this is a clear signal to those around you that you do not wish to be disturbed. Furthermore, you may find it helpful to set some type of timer as when you get into the zone while being mindful it can be easy to lose track of time.

With the preliminaries out of the way, the first thing that you are going to want to do is to plant your feet firmly a comfortable distance apart from one another whether you are standing or sitting. If standing, take care that you are in a place where you can easily keep your balance. With your feet firmly planted slowly stretch out your body so that you assume the proper posture for your current surroundings. Take a moment to feel your body move with the rhythm of the train/bus and consider how you are connected not just to the transportation you are riding but to all of those who are sharing the journey with you.

Once you feel that you are centered, choose a spot in front of you that is approximately three feet from your current position. Choose a spot that is close to the ground, perhaps just a foot or two above the floor of the bus or train. Slowly lower your eyes to this point on the ground without lowering your neck, it is important to maintain proper posture throughout the exercise. As you feel your eyes begin to dip towards the floor focus exclusively on all of the sensory information they are providing you. From there, slowly incorporate the sensations that are being provided by the rest of your senses.

In order to tune out all of the noise and movement that naturally comes with riding public transportation, focus on your breathing and concentrate on taking rhythmic deep breaths at a nice slow pace.

Once you have found a rhythm that works for you consider one of the options below as a means of focusing your attention and attaining a state of mindfulness that might not seem possible otherwise. Remember, practicing mindfulness meditation while using public transportation is even trickier to get the hang of than the other types of mindfulness meditation discussed in these pages. Don't get discouraged if you can't clear your mind as easily as you may be able to elsewhere, as with any other skill practice makes perfect.

Ways to focus your attention

Depending on the quality of your ride, you may find that the sensation of movement that you are experiencing to be enough to allow you to focus on the moment. Your body will be constantly moving in this situation, providing you with plenty of sensations to focus on. If you have to move around during your trip consider focusing on the similarities and differences that the two positions provide you. As you breathe deeply feel the movement coursing beneath your feet, up through your body and all the way to your arms. Use each stop as an opportunity to refocus yourself on the moment. Don't forget to pay enough attention to your other senses that you lose track of your stop!

Depending on the quality of your public transportation, you may find that smell is another great anchor to plant you firmly in the present. This is also great practice for taking in sensations without judging them as you are likely to smell plenty of things that are good as well as bad while utilizing public transportation. Rather than making judgement calls regarding particular smells, simply focus on each unique smell as it appears, without breaking out of the rhythm of your breathing.

If the public transportation that you are on is particularly raucous, or if you don't have any other way to keep track of how close you are to your stop, you can count the number of stops you have remaining and repeat the number over and over again in your mind until it forms a type of mantra. This method of keeping in touch with the moment can also be combined with one of the others for maximum effectiveness.

While on one hand, practicing mindfulness meditation while surrounded by so many people can present its own unique challenges, on the other hand it also provides you with a breadth of different sensory information that you are unlikely to get when practicing any other type of mindfulness meditation, including practicing during your commute. Instead of trying to tune everything around you out completely, a more effective choice is to embrace the chaos that surrounds you and use it as a way to drown out any particularly nagging thoughts that have been plaguing you.

Consider the other passengers for example, are they talking to other passengers, ask yourself what they look like, how they act, sound, smell etc. Each stop provides a host of new ways to focus your attention and thus remain in the moment easier. What's more you have more sensations to focus on as well. Focus on the temperature changes as you move along your route as that and any other sensations are likely to change at a moment's notice.

Chapter 9: Mind Your Breathing

One of the first ways you can learn to practice mindfulness is through how you breathe. Also known as mindfulness, deep, or meditative breathing, it has been scientifically shown to be very effective in helping people relax their way to significantly improved mental and physical health and well being. Mindfulness breathing is a very excellent way to channel your thoughts on the present or current moment without the need to evaluate them as either right or wrong. As such, mindfulness breathing allows you to trigger your body and mind's relaxation response, which is of great value when it comes to winning the war on depression, anxiety and stress.

But why is mindful breathing helpful in this war? Mindfulness breathing is able to help you deactivate that area of your nervous system that triggers the production of stress hormones — the sympathetic nervous system. Pretty cool, huh? Also, mindfulness breathing helps your body turn on its parasympathetic nervous system, which is responsible for shutting down that which pumps stress hormones all throughout your body. By turning off and turning on the sympathetic and parasympathetic nervous systems, respectively, you trigger your body to relax, slow down your heart rate, and bring down blood pressure every time you feel anxious and stressed. You'll experience calmness as a result.

For these to happen, your brain must be at its peak performance. And what helps your brain be at its peak? Yes, it's air or oxygen, which is why mindfulness breathing is very crucial for peak mental health, e.g., beating depression, anxiety and stress.

BREATHING EXERCISES

So how does it look like to breathe mindfully? Try doing this exercise so you can learn how to breathe mindfully:

Set aside 2 minutes daily for practicing mindfulness breathing. Make a commitment to yourself to do this because otherwise, you won't learn mindfulness breathing.

Decide on a place where you will regularly practice mindfulness breathing. Make sure it's a place where you won't be disturbed during practice and will be able to sit comfortably. If you're employed, consider practicing in a rarely used room, a nearby park, or if you have your own office – your room. If you're a student, consider the library (the best because it's supposed to be a quiet place), a chapel in the campus, or in your room (if you occupy it alone). If you're a housewife, consider one of your home's spare rooms and if you don't have one, the bathroom!

Decide a particular time of the day in which you'll practice mindfulness breathing. It's best to choose a time when everybody else is asleep (if practicing at home) or your officemates or classmates haven't arrived yet (if at the office or in school). It helps minimize risk of being disturbed. No people, no disturbance.

To begin, sit with your body upright and place both your hands down the sides of your body or with palms facing up and open, on top of your thighs.

Close your eyes – and keep it that way throughout the exercise – and smile a half-smile. Believe me, the smile is relevant.

Breathe in deeply. Breathe in through your nose, making sure you breathe using your belly and not your chest. You'll know if you're belly-breathing if your tummy expands as you breathe in. Your chest shouldn't go up as you do. Otherwise, you're chest breathing.

Hold your breath for 1 second before exhaling through your mouth. Once you've fully exhaled the air out, hold your breath for 1 second before breathing in again in the same manner. Repeat multiple times.

As you practice this, don't be surprised to find your mind trying to and eventually wandering off. When this happens, simply acknowledge that it did and just let your thoughts drift away as if it were smoke being blown by the wind or a log drifting downstream on a river. As soon as the thoughts drift away, refocus your mind and attention on your breath. Whenever you become distracted with thoughts, simply let them drift away and refocus on your breathing.

As a beginner, it's expected that you'll find this simple practice to be quite difficult in the beginning. Don't worry – it's normal. One way you can remain focused or refocus on your breathing is by using a mantra, which is a word or phrase that you say repeatedly. Mantras function as some sort of mental anchor that helps you stay focused on your breathing. A good example of a mindfulness breathing mantra is "breathe in, breathe out."

After doing this for several minutes already, feel free to open your eyes again.

If by any chance you feel dizzy after opening your eyes, just let the dizziness fade away before attempting to stand up. You don't need to worry because your dizziness is but an indication that your blood pressure went down as a result of the relaxation effects of mindfulness breathing. Upon ending your mindfulness breathing exercise, you breathe normally again and your blood pressure starts normalizing again.

If you're wondering whether or not you can overdo this, the answer is no. You can do this as frequently as you like during the day anytime and anywhere. The important thing is that you do it at least once daily, staring with a 2-minute duration. As you become more and more accustomed to the practice, you can gradually increasing your mindfulness breathing duration to 5 minutes or up to 30 minutes! The longer the duration becomes, the more victories you'll experience over depression, anxiety, and stress.

Chapter 10: Other Mindfulness Exercises For Kids

Engaging all the senses is just one part of mindfulness. The other part is learning to be aware of what is going on around you and inside you. The exercises here can be combined with those that focus the senses. Some will help your child learn to describe their emotions, while others will be useful tools to release those emotions and accompanying thoughts. You should vary the exercises that you practice each day, so your child develops a wide range of skills.

Squish and Release

"Lie down on your back and put your hands at your sides. Breathe in and watch your belly fill up. Then, watch your belly move down as you push the air out. Practice tightening your muscles by squeezing your fingers and toes. One, two, three, four, five. Now, let go. Breathe in, breathe out."

"Now, use the same squishing technique to squish the rest of your body. Make the muscles in your feet and legs tight, ball and squeeze your fists, and push your shoulders up toward your ears. Try to make a smaller, more squished version of yourself. Then, let go and let your hands and feet relax on the floor. You should feel tingling over your whole body. Focus on this moment and know that it is teaching you to feel everything, wherever you are. "

The Mind Jar

A mind jar is meant to help a child settle their mind. It is a visual representation of what our mind goes through when we are upset, and then when calm ourselves. You can create a mind jar with your child using water, glitter, beads, seashells, or anything else that you want to use. Place the objects in a glass jar or plastic bottle. When your child is upset, ask them to shake the jar.

"See how everything is floating around the jar? It is upset and chaotic. This is your sadness or anger upsetting your mind. Now, watch and see what happens. Notice how everything is settling down. The jar is starting to become calm. Imagine all your bad thoughts are calming down and settling on the bottom of the jar."

Breathing Buddies

"Take your favorite stuffed animal and find somewhere to lie down. Place the stuffed animal on your tummy. Breathe in, breathe out. Watch your stuffed animal move up and down. Is there pressure on your tummy? What else do you feel? Do you feel in your tummy or tingling in your fingers?"

"If you are feeling bad or sad or angry, use the bubbles to help you release bad thoughts. As you breathe in and your stuffed animal is pushed outward, pretend you are collecting good thoughts. When you breathe out and your stuffed animal moves closer to you, pretend that they are pushing out all the bad with your air."

Describing Emotions

A major element of mindfulness is being able to understand your emotions. Have your child lie down and close their eyes. Remind them that you are not going to judge them. Then, ask:

"What are you feeling right now?

How do you know you are feeling that emotion?

What does that feeling feel like?

Can you feel the emotion on your face?

Does the emotion feel good or bad?"

"If you don't like the way you are feeling, think about what you can do to stop the emotion. Practice squishing your body and letting go of the emotion or picture the bad thoughts as bubbles and watch them float away."

By practicing this in a non-confrontational, calm setting, your child will learn how to deal with negative emotions in public too.

The Weather Report

Another way to help your child experience their emotions in a non-judgmental way is to have them give a weather report. For example, a tsunami, volcano, or thunderstorm might represent anger and sunshine might represent happiness.

"Can you color/draw a picture of what you are experiencing? What do the clouds mean? What does the sunshine mean? Would you like the weather to change?"

It is important to let your child describe the weather to you. Do not interpret their weather, because weather is something that can have different meanings. For example, a thunderstorm could represent anger or sadness. Clouds could represent sad and gloomy, but they could also represent boredom.

Noticing the Heart

Whether you are sleeping, running and playing, or taking a test, your heart is beating on. Your heartbeat can say a lot about what you are feeling. Calm emotions cause a slower heartbeat, while anger, stress, or other emotions can make your heart beat faster. Physical stress can also make your heart beat faster.

"Lie down on the floor and practice breathing. Put your hand over your heart and feel it beat. Then, stand up and run in place or do jumping jacks for a full minute. Now, place your hand over your heart and feel it moving fast. Notice how your breathing has changed.

Then, close your eyes. Can you feel your heartbeat pounding in your ears or your head? What else do you feel? Is there any tingling or squirming in your body?"

Take a Noticing Walk

Walking is a great physical activity, but it also a good time to take the time to notice everything around you. You also don't need any equipment. As you walk with your child, ask them to point out things using their senses. For example, they might notice the colors of a bush of flowers that you walk by, but also the smell.

"What do you see that attracts your eye? Now, take a moment to notice the blades of grass blowing in the wind. Do you see how the wind shakes the tree leaves? What can you smell? Does it smell pleasant? What sounds do you hear? What do you think the asphalt would feel like if you were barefoot?"

Asking questions like these will get your child noticing the many things in the world around them. Often, these will be things they have taken for granted in the past.

Chapter 11: Mindfulness And Inner Awareness

One of the biggest benefits of living life mindfully is that your inner awareness awakens. Well, there is another way of putting this sentence because the reverse is also true. When you begin to awaken your inner awareness you are very likely to lead a life filled with mindfulness. Therefore, mindfulness and inner awareness are inextricably intertwined with each other. So, what is inner awareness?

Many of us are uncertain of who we truly are. Yes, we do have a job, a family, we have relationships, we are part of a certain community, etc. Yet, deep down there is a lot of confusion and we don't know our true selves. We are unsure of what our purpose is. When you come across this kind of satiation where inner powerlessness is gnawing at you, you are invariably affected by some or all of the following symptoms:

You become obsessed with goals and you want to accomplish things constantly

You become attached to certain things or to a certain group of people

You are constantly under the strain of an internal struggle that never seems to end

You want to try out everything so that you feel you are in control of your life

You are obsessed with earning money or being around a particular cadre of people to feel worthy of yourself. You feel you are nothing if this doesn't happen

All these symptoms reflect a missing link deep inside you. You are unsure of what that missing link is but you know that gaping hole in your self is simply not filling up. You feel unsettled at times even as you struggle to fill up that hole with materialistic things, which only seem to make the gap even bigger than before. This kind of life brings with it nothing but stress, anxiety, and unhappiness.

As your inner awareness remains hidden somewhere in the depths of your mind, you feel like you are running around in circles with nowhere to go. There is a sense of being purposeless and directionless because despite achieving outward success in all your endeavors, there is still something nagging you. You lead your life in a mindless manner.

So, how do you awaken your inner awareness so that you can become more mindful or how can you become more mindful so that you can awaken your inner awareness? If you get one right, the other will fall into place. Let us look at some ways to help you in this direction.

Question Your Emotions

When you feel any negative emotion such as anger, resentment, boredom, depression, etc., question your emotions. For example, ask yourself some questions like:

Why am I feeling anger?

Why do I feel depressed?

Why do I feel so much of hurt?

It is important to remember at this point that other people do not make you angry. People and their actions are only triggers for your emotions. The way you respond and react to the triggered emotion is up to you and not up to the circumstance and people outside of you. Those emerging emotions are trying to tell you something. Instead of reacting to them, listen to their story and you will find yourself being awakened. Let us try and find probable answers one of the above example questions that you asked yourself.

Why Am I Feeling Anger?

Why does one get angry? Constantly feeling angry can be very frustrating both for yourself and for the people you work and live with. One of the best places to try and find a solution for your anger is to find the reason behind the rather debilitating emotion. So, when you feel angry, step back from your emotion and ask yourself. "Why am I so upset and angry?"

If the answer that comes out is something like, "I am angry because my spouse didn't do what I asked,' then it is a shallow answer because if it is something so small, then the anger will not be so repetitive and debilitating. It will disappear after some time. You simply are not digging deeper into your mind for truth and, perhaps, unpleasant answers to this question.

Moreover, even if your spouse didn't do what you asked, the anger is your response and not his or hers. How to handle that? Your reaction to the trigger of anger is what you need to look at. Anything that happens remains as it happens until you give it a label as being 'good,' 'bad,' or 'neutral.' This choice invariably is decided by the emotion you feel at that moment in time. So, you must ask yourself, "Why am I choosing anger as a response to a situation?"

The reason for choosing could be different for different people and for different situations. That is the answer you need to find. The answers you get will facilitate the awakening of your inner awareness. Anger is actually a mask that covers up the true emotions whether it be jealousy, lack of confidence, helplessness, or anything else. Find that root cause and find solutions for that cause and you will be able to handle your anger without nastily reacting to it.

Use this same method to find true answers for other questions that you asked yourself with regard to your emotions.

Question Your Thoughts

Look at your thoughts objectively and like a witness without being judgmental about them. Look at how your thoughts are making you react in a particular way. Ask yourself questions that are bound to give you illuminating answers:

Are your thoughts and the actions of those driving thoughts a result of a restrictive habit or a limited belief?

Are you trying to manipulate something or someone to behave in a particular way based on how you are reacting to the thoughts that are coming up with respect to that situation or person?

What is your true intention behind all those confusing thoughts and the actions they drive? Why are you doing something in a specific way?

Are there ways of doing things differently from the current way of doing things? For example, is it imperative to do a job you hate because of having to meet your monthly expenses? Are there other options you can try out there?

How much of your past thoughts are ruling over your present?

What are the limiting beliefs and valueless preconditions that can easily be let go? How different will your life be if you do this?

When you question your thoughts instead of responding or reacting to them, you become a mere witness with no attachment to them. You will notice these thoughts will rise, reach a peak, and sometimes simply vanish into thin air. Don't let these temperate elements take over your life.

Let Go of Restrictive Elements

Stop struggling with yourself and let go of things that are holding you back. In fact, the ultimate action would be to let go of everything in your life. You will notice that only the true purpose will remain. Letting go works like the distillation of water; taking away all impurities so that you are left with only pure and nourishing elixir of life.

Be Inspired and Monitor your Actions

Always find ways to inspire and motivate yourself. There are plenty of resources out there. Find inspiring books to read. Meet and talk to people who have done well for themselves (not necessarily in terms of materialistic success). Join a support group. Believe me, there are many people wanting help and helping others find their meaning in life will help you find your own.

Keep track of your actions. Monitor them so that you are acutely aware of how you are responding or reacting to situations and/or people. Watch yourself do things. Are you too caught up with watching TV or on social media or socializing more than needed? Listen to your inner voice.

Dig deep inside of your mind to find out what is it that you want from life? Some answers may be unpleasant, but mostly the answers will be liberating. Overcome fear and find solutions to your problems. Don't be bogged down by life without truly understanding what your true purpose in life. Get a hold of yourself, awaken your inner awareness, and lead a more fulfilling and mindful life than before.

Most importantly, learn to forgive. Forgive yourself for the past mistakes and move forward. You will find the wherewithal to forgive others their mistakes too. Forgiveness is the most important and, perhaps, the most difficult step in creating inner awareness. Find that strength for forgiveness.

Chapter 12: Benefits Of Mindfulness Meditation

The world of today is undoubtedly a busy and taxing one. A mother has to keep one eye on her kids while the other on the television. An office worker plans his day while commuting to his work and then planning his weekend. Thus, many people who are in a rush to accomplish their tasks find themselves losing connection with the present moment. They usually miss out on what they are doing as well as how they are feeling. They even fail to notice if they feel well-rested when they wake up or simply observe their surroundings on their way to work.

Mindfulness involves focusing your attention deliberately on the present moment and at the same time accepting it without opinions or judgments. In fact, mindfulness is considered as a key factor in attaining happiness.

Buddhism is said to be the root of the cultivation of mindfulness. However, many religions have included some forms of prayer technique, which aid in shifting one's thoughts away from his normal or habitual preoccupations to appreciating the present moment as well as a broader perspective about life.

Based on the ancient roots of mindfulness meditation, the founder and former director of the Stress Reduction Clinic, professor emeritus Jon Kabat-Zinn, helped in bringing the mindfulness meditation practice into modern medicine. He showed that improvements in both the physical and psychological symptoms are achieved through the practice of mindfulness. In addition, the professor emeritus said that mindfulness meditation results in positive changes in health behaviors and attitudes.

Kabat-Zinn also described mindfulness as the practice of paying attention to the present moment and at the same time letting go of opinions and judgments like one's life depends on it. He said that human beings only have one real moment, which is the present. Moreover, he said that one's life may depend on the present moment.

There are various benefits of practicing mindfulness meditation. For one, most people who have tried a mindfulness meditation session claim that it reduces stress. According to a research published in the Health Psychology journal, mindfulness is associated with decreasing not only the stress itself but the levels of the stress hormone known as cortisol.

It is also said that mindfulness meditation changes and protects the brain. In recent years, research showed that a mindfulness meditation technique referred to as integrative body-mind training can cause changes in the brain, which may protect it from mental illness. The meditation practice was associated with greater signaling connections in the brain known as axonal density and increased **myelin**, a protective tissue surrounding the axons in the brain's anterior cingulate region.

Mindfulness meditation lets one discover his true self. According to a study, mindfulness meditation helps in overcoming common "blind spots" that either increase or decrease one's flaws beyond reality. It aids in helping an individual see and analyze himself objectively.

Mindfulness meditation makes an individual a better person. More often than not, people who attend meditation session feel fulfilled with the things that meditation does for them. However, they fail to recognize that mindfulness meditation may also be beneficial to other individuals whom they interact with. This is because during mindfulness meditation, a person becomes kinder and more compassionate as he notice current experiences as they are without judgments, but with acceptance. Research done at Harvard University and Northeastern University showed that meditation is associated with behavior which is inclined to doing good.

Some people may not truly understand the value of mindfulness meditation. Apart from those already mentioned above, it still has other benefits. Among them is that mindfulness meditation can increase the "caps" at the end of one's genes known as telomerase. These "caps" are responsible for prolonging one's life as well as reducing damage in one's cells. Moreover, research found out that mindfulness supports one's immune system, which makes the body fight off both common and chronic diseases, including flu and cancer.

During mindfulness meditation, one's concentration is improved and pensive thinking is reduced. More often than not, deep-thinking causes high levels of stress, which is almost inevitable in today's society. Apart from being mental health hazards, stress and pensive thinking are the symptoms that lead individuals to seek assistance from therapists.

Mindfulness meditation is proven as a great tool for mental health professionals. It is a tool used in helping people understand, deal, and tolerate their emotions in positive and healthy ways. It allows an individual to change his habitual responses through pausing and choosing how he acts. When a person is mindful, he is able to experience life as he lives it. He is able to experience the world right through his five senses. A person who is mindful is able to taste the food he eats and acknowledge the thoughts he is thinking about. In turn, he learns how his minds work and is able to label his feelings and thoughts better rather than allowing them to prevail and dictate his actions and behavior.

Given that mindfulness meditation is an efficient way to know oneself, to live in the present moment, and to reduce stress, cultivating or fostering mindfulness is indeed a powerful tool in therapy. Research showed that therapists practicing mindfulness themselves have better understanding and results with their patients even if mindfulness techniques are not used during their therapy sessions. All the same, incorporating mindfulness into therapy is a proven tool when it comes to treating a number of common mental health problems.

As mindfulness meditation and practices was integrated to some mental-related therapies, such as Dialectical Behavioral Therapy (DBT), it led to positive outcomes. It is being applied more and more to other types of therapy and has further established that it can help in treating people who suffer with bipolar and other personality disorders. It is also said that mindfulness can reduce the possibility of recurring depression. As such, it was also incorporated in clinical practice as numerous therapists found it to produce positive results.

Teaching an individual mindfulness practices helps in training his mind to notice his own feelings, sensations, and thoughts objectively. People who teach mindfulness practices and meditation should do so with kindness and compassion given that most people are inclined to losing patience with themselves, specifically in the initial stages of trying out mindfulness meditation.

As an individual learns to live in the moment and lets go of judgment, he increases his mental agility and regulates his emotions better.

A Summary of the Benefits of Mindfulness Meditation

Well-Being

As an individual increases his/her capacity for mindfulness, he/she is able to support a number of attitudes, which contributes or leads to a fulfilled life. Becoming mindful also makes it easier for an individual to relish life's pleasures as they happen; creates a greater capacity when dealing with adverse situations; and helps in becoming fully committed in activities.

Given that mindfulness has its primary focus in the present moment, people who practice it are able to avoid getting caught up in regrets over the past or worries about the future. People who are mindful become less preoccupied with concerns about self-esteem as well as success. Moreover, they are able to establish deeper and better connections with others.

Mental Health

Mindfulness meditation is said to improve one's mental health. Psychotherapists have utilized mindfulness meditation in recent years as an integral factor in the treatment of several mental or psychological problems. These include anxiety disorders, depression, eating disorders, conflicts between couples, substance abuse, and obsessive-compulsive disorder (OCD).

Physical Health

Mindfulness meditation also aids in improving one's physical health. Scientists have discovered that mindfulness techniques aid in improving physical health in several ways. These include treating heart disease, relieving stress, reducing high levels of blood pressure, improving sleep, reducing chronic pain, and alleviating gastrointestinal difficulties.

According to some experts, mindfulness meditation is able to help people when it comes to accepting their own experiences, such as painful emotions, instead of reacting with avoidance and aversion.

Today, the integration of mindfulness meditation with psychotherapy is becoming a common process, specifically in cognitive behavioral therapy. Most experts find this development sensible given that meditation and cognitive behavioral therapy have the same goal of assisting individuals gain position on maladaptive, self-defeating, and irrational thoughts.

Chapter 13: Why Practice Mindfulness

All of our challenges in life, without exception, are relational. In other words, a problem cannot exist in isolation; it can only exist if we have a personal identification with it. If we hear of a person of whom we do not know, who is experiencing life-threatening injuries, we will not consider it a challenge for us. If the person with life-threatening injuries happens to be us or someone we love, then we will most likely feel challenged by it. From the perspective of deeper levels of consciousness, the person with the life-threatening injuries, and our own sense of identity are nothing more than forms of thought.

Practicing mindfulness is important if we are to understand the true nature of existence, which is consciousness. We need to practice mindfulness so that we can discern our thoughts, emotions, and sensations and observe them without identifying with them. When we become skillful in mindfulness, we can enjoy a new found freedom. All of our problems will gradually fade away. They will fade away because we will no longer identify them, which only prolong their existence. You will find yourself happier and more effective in your daily life. The reason for this is that you will lose your sense of identification with thought; your sense of identity will become increasingly established in what is referred to as your Buddha nature, or pure consciousness.

A lack of mindfulness is the reason for violence and destruction against others and our planet. In short, anything we do that cause injury to ourselves, others, or nature, is the result of not being mindful. To be mindful is to be fully aware of ourselves and our connection to all of life. To not live mindfully is to live a life where limited attention is given to what is most important, the here and now.

Lifting the Veil of Illusions

Our world is full of illusions. More accurately, our minds create illusions of the world. These illusions seem so real to us that we rarely question them.

When we gaze at a star, we believe that it currently exists, though this is not accurate. The star that we are looking at may have burned out hundreds or even thousands of years ago. Because of its vast distance from Earth, it takes this span of time for its light to travel close enough for us to observe it.

When we view the world around us, we see color. The grass is green; the sky is blue, there are red sports cars, and there are black cats; however, all these things are actually colorless; they only appear to have a color. Light has various colored wavelengths: Red, yellow, green, and blue. When light shines on an object, those wavelengths that are not absorbed by the object will be reflected off it. A red sports car appears to be red because all the wavelengths are absorbed by the car, except for the red wavelength. The red wavelength is reflected off the car and perceived by our eyes, giving the impression that the car is red.

The planet we live on is both round and continuously orbiting the sun at high speeds, yet we experience the world as flat and motionless.

If you snap your fingers, you may think that the snapping sound and the act of snapping your fingers occur at the same time; however, this is incorrect. Light travels at a faster speed than sound, so the observing of the snapping action is received by the brain before the sound of the snap reaches your ears. The illusion that these things are happening at the same time is the result of the brain making adjustments for the differences when the sensory information is received by you.

A brick seems solid, yet at the atomic level, a physicist will tell you that the brick's true composition is that of energy and subatomic particles separated by vast distances of space.

The brain is unable to distinguish between an imagined object and one that is observed. Your brain cannot tell the difference between a rose that you are observing in a garden from a rose that you are visualizing in your mind.

These are just a few examples of illusions that we experience on a daily basis. While these examples of illusions may seem to have little consequence for our lives, there are others that have a profound impact on our emotional well-being:

Impermanency

One of the most important teachings of the Buddha has to do with impermanence. In fact, the root of humanity's suffering is created by it. This illusion is one of the primary causes of war, violence, unhappiness, or a lack of fulfillment. But before we can understand impermanence, we first need to examine the role that the conditioning of our society has on the way we view our world and ourselves.

From the time we were small children, we were conditioned to focus on the world outside of ourselves. An infant knows from its first day that its survival is dependent on its parents. It looks toward its parents for nourishment, comfort, affection, and protection. The child learns that it needs to appease its parents to get their approval. To not appease its parents could result in disapproval and the inability to gain what it desires.

This outward focus expands as we progress through life. We focus on school, our teachers, our friends, our employers, our peer group, the media, and our culture. We become very aware on what others are doing, what they think of us, and how we can fit in. At the same time, our society does not encourage us to explore our inner world, to understand our emotions and feelings, how to express them or to get to know ourselves.

In short, our socialization leads to the typical person lacking a sense of self, a sense of self that is free from the expectations, approval, and disapproval of others. Our sense of self-worth frequently is dependent on the conditions that lie outside our self. Examples of such conditions include the people we know, how much money we make, the work we do, our role in the family, our possessions, our physical appearance, how we dress, the music we listen to, where we live, and so on.

It is this kind of outward focus that leads to most of our sufferings and problems. The reason for this goes to the principle of impermanence, which states all phenomenal

aspects of life are an illusion. Anything that we can see, smell, hear, touch, measure, or weigh is considered phenomenal, meaning, all of the experience is phenomenal. The world of phenomena is considered an illusion because it is impermanent as it is constantly changing; it cannot be depended on. Relationships come and go; money is gained and lost; our possession will eventually break or be lost; we can lose our jobs; our physical appearance will change with age; our bodies will break down, and the people we know will die. The phenomenal world also exists within us. Our thoughts, our beliefs, our emotions, and our feelings are also in constant flux.

We have learned to focus on the outer world to acquire what we desire or need, be it material goods or the approval of others, yet this same world is uncertain and constantly changing. To depend on that which cannot be depended upon is the cause of all of our problems. Practicing mindfulness can lead to the revealing of that aspect of our life which is non-phenomenal, that part of us that never changes, that part of us which is eternal.

Illusions of Separation

With our outward focus comes the illusion of separation. Most of the problems that humanity faces are the result of not seeing the oneness of our lives with our environment. To see our world today is to see how, as a species, we have lacked understanding of this. This lack of understanding is evident almost everywhere that we look. War, the destruction of our planet, and social injustice are just a few examples of our ignorance.

You and your surroundings are not two separate things; they are intimately connected. There are numerous examples of this relationship. A person who is depressed stops cleaning his or her living quarters. As their living quarters become increasingly untidy, it further adds to their sense of unhappiness. A company pollutes the surrounding area with toxic materials, which in turn leads to the people in the area developing cancer and other illnesses. A family has a spouse that engages in disruptive activities such as substance abuse, excessive drinking, having an affair or gambling. The consequences of these activities can destroy the family unit. These activities are forms of karma. Karma is not restricted to the individual as karma is shared among those around us. Beliefs and behaviors are propagated among populations, cultures, or families. Nothing that we think, say or do escapes the detection of the universe. Whatever we do, it will have an effect on our surroundings, and the consequences will return to us.

The Present Moment

The present moment contains all moments. If we learn to establish ourselves in the present moment awareness, we will be able to access all of existence. From the perspective of causation, every moment is the result of the previous moment. The present moment is the culmination of all causes made in the previous moment, while the seeds of the future lie in the present moment.

The future is the culmination of all causes made in the present moment. In this manner, both past and future are contained in the present moment. To live in mindfulness is to be the witness of the unlimited potential that is contained in every moment.

For us to not me mindful in the present moment is to remain blind to the essential causes for our life's unfolding. It is for this reason why we distract ourselves as previously described. Rather than becoming mindful of the present moment, we engage in the endless pursuit of happiness and fulfillment, which can never be reached as we are in pursuit of the illusions of happiness and fulfillment. They are the illusions of happiness and fulfillment because they are transient.

Everything we experience in life is impermanent. Relationships, health, physical appearance, titles, status, money, and possessions are constantly changing and will at some point fade from existence. Even when they present themselves to our life, we cannot be fully mindful of them as our minds are directed toward the future or the past.

When we develop mindfulness, we create a profound transformation in our lives where we develop a completely new relationship with our thoughts, feelings, emotions, and perceptions. Even more profoundly, we develop a new sense of identity that is no longer based on these phenomena. We come to the realization that we are not our thoughts, feelings, emotions, and perceptions; rather, we are the observer of these phenomena. We still experience them, but they no longer will have the power to control our lives.

Chapter 14: Streamlining Your Obligations

A great way to reduce mental clutter is to limit your obligations to things that don't matter that much. For example, stressing over a school bake sale when your heart just isn't in the cause doesn't make much sense. Yes, you love your kids, but are you really helping them, or any of the kids with the hundred dollars raised? Could your time be better spent elsewhere?

There will always be things we don't want to do and have to do, but there are bigger reasons behind them. For example, while you may not like your job, you go because you need to pay the bills, so your family has somewhere to live. Crossing that line becomes working overtime and exhausting yourself so your kids can have the latest and greatest toys. There is a fine line between necessary and excessive.

Tapping into your inner desires and what really drives you is a great way to streamline your obligations. Take a look at each thing that you do on a daily, weekly and monthly basis and assess whether or not it suits your ultimate purpose. It's okay to be a little selfish here. Remember that self-care is crucial to being an active, beneficial person to others. If you feel that other people's wellness comes before yours, you are missing the point. This is your life, and if you are not happy, you're not doing it right!

Start by making a list of things that you are responsible for. Break them into different categories. Physically write them in different columns. Put things like work under the essential category, a collection of things you need to do to keep a roof over your head and food on the table. This will include things like work, travel for work, grocery shopping, cooking, cleaning the house, and the like.

Look at the things you do less often, and figure out where they fit. Maybe you care for a family member in your spare time, or you drive the neighborhood kids to school every day as a favor to their parents. These are things that aren't necessary to life but are driven more by your morals and values.

Determine whether or not each activity fits in to your moral conscience, or if it has just become something that is expected from you. If you are doing more things because you feel you have to than out of an actual moral need to do them, it is time to look at these events. Could you split carpool with another neighbor to take some of the responsibility off your shoulders? Why does it all have to fall on you?

Next, assess how much time you spend on each of these tasks. Is the majority of your time doing things that are necessary, and only a little bit spent on self-care and fun? Yes, you will probably spend quite a bit of time at work, and financially, it probably doesn't make sense to up and leave your job.

However, is it possible to cut your work down? Maybe you volunteer for special projects at work to try and get ahead. Would that extra time be better utilized at home with your family? Off on an adventure? Can you delegate tasks to others so that responsibility for some things can be shared? Lots of people end up being a martyr for their cause because they feel obligated to do work themselves. All you gain is less time to do what you really want to do.

What you can do is decide how to create more balance between the need-to-dos and the want-to-dos. Striking a good balance means you are living your life responsibly, but also making the most out of the moments you don't need to be working.

That's the safe way to go, and you know it. However, the next step may derail that thought process altogether. Yes, you can fit more fun, excitement, and meaning into your hours off the clock, but if the negativity that ensues during your work hours outweighs even the greatest days off the clock, you have a problem. It is vital that you be honest with yourself in this process, and it may relate to more than just work. Are you best friends with your grade school bestie because you still love them, or has the relationship gone south? Do you raise your kids with your spouse because you want to, or because you feel obligated to?

It is and will be difficult to come to terms with some of the decisions you have made, and it is up to you to listen to your conscience for guidance here. Keep listening to those subtle cues your conscience gives you. Use this inner wisdom to guide the decisions, twists, and turns in your life.

Finally, don't be so nervous about the financial side of life. We often get so bogged down with being in the green that we forget there is much more to life than money. Yes, it can create stability by paying for a safe and warm home, food to feed the family, and even fund vacations and adventures. However, lots of people forgo these fun things because they are busy working to make that money. They don't have time to take these adventures.

Assessing your obligations can be a daunting process, something that doesn't need to be dealt with all at once. Take it a day at a time and simply try to find balance in that day. For example, if you know you are working eight hours, what can you do in the other eight hours you won't be spending sleeping? There is quite a bit of time to be utilized, and you can certainly balance the work with some fun.

Starting each day with a bit of self-reflection and meditation can help your day get off on the right foot. Just take a few minutes to ask yourself what you want out of this day. How can you incorporate things into your day to make that vision a reality? What can you do today that will bring you one step closer to the life you live in your dreams? Life is about small bits of progress, you don't have to uproot your entire life to be happy.

Chapter 15: Practicing Mindfulness In The Twenty-First Century

In this information age – often the digital technology makes it more challenging to live a mindful life. In this chapter, we are going to discuss how you can combine mindful practice while using digital technology.

Following are a few ways to create digital downtime. The approach is based on how much time you have available:

A few minutes: When working, take a few minutes break every hour. Every hour take a step back, take a few gentle, deep breaths and walk a few steps.

A few hours: Once you finished your office hours, take a break from the screen. It is becoming a familiar scenario that people work all day in front of a screen and then go back home and relax by watching another screen. Refresh yourself by taking up a hobby, participating in a sport, socializing or doing a spot of mindfulness practice.

A few days: Maintain a routine and take time off from technology every week. If possible, aim for at least one day off. During your off day, avoid checking your emails or social media, leave your phone behind and do something more natural and energizing.

A few weeks: Ideally you should take a few weeks break yearly. During your holidays, try to spend an extended period of time away from your laptop, phones and so on. This will help your creative juices to flow naturally and your mind will come up with unique solutions for challenging work place decisions.

Emailing Mindfully

Emailing is popular, it is both extremely convenient and incredibly stressful. Here are a few tips for you to emailing mindfully:

Make a brief emailing plan: Use a notebook and write down who you want to send emails and a few brief points of your emails each day. Then write your emails first and check your emails later. Making a plan and writing them down only takes a few minutes, but it will help you to save hours of time sifting through, reading and replying emails that aren't important.

Watch out for email addiction: Unless your job is checking emails, fix one or two dedicated times for checking emails. Fixing a time for checking email will impose discipline on your life, help you focus on what is in front of you rather than wasting time with unnecessary messages.

Breathe before sending: Take three mindful breaths before sending each email. This practice will help you become more mindful, you get the time to reflect on what you have written and stay focused on the task.

See your emails from a different perspective: Once you have taken the mindful breaths, think how the receiver will react after receiving your mail.

Reviewing may promote you to edit some parts or you may decide to call instead.

One positive email daily: Build a habit of sending at least positive emails daily. Habitually focusing on the positives helps to rebalance your brain's usual negativity bias and helps you to feel better. Praise a new employee for doing given task efficiently, thank your boss for excepting your delayed report, or congratulate your coworker on her sales presentation.

Control your emails, avoid the reverse: Build a habit that leads to you controlling your emails, and doesn't let your emails controlling you.

Among other things, you can turn off your message notifications to avoid distractions.

Phone Mindfully

You need to be aware of several things with mindful phoning

What the caller or receiver is saying

The tone of their voice

Your state of mind

The things that you want to say

Why you are calling or want to achieve from the conversation

How can you help the other person

The next time you make a phone call, try this exercise:

Take a few moments to be mindful. Take a short mindful pause by feeling your bodily sensations, your breathing or connecting with one of your senses.

Write down the goal of your conversation. It will only take a few seconds.

Stand up. You work all day sitting in front of a computer, phone time gives you an opportunity to stand up and a walk a few paces.

Listen. Listen more than you speak. Focus on their actual words as well as the other person's tone of the voice.

Be aware of your emotions: If the phone conversation makes you uncomfortable, anxious or worried, notice the feeling in your body. With your breathing, feel the emotion, then speak from your wise mind instead of reacting. Try to go into greater levels of mindfulness as the conversation continues. This approach will help you stay calm and avoid saying things that you will regret later.

End the conversation when you feel it's time. Don't drag it out unnecessarily.

Before phoning, do a short mindful exercise. This will help you stay more focused during the conversation.

Using your smartphone mindfully

If you think you need to control your smartphone habits, then try these steps:

Be conscious: When you find yourself looking at your beloved iPhone or have the desire to check your emails, ask yourself what emotions you are feeling. Worried, stressed, boredom, anxiety or perhaps loneliness?

Be disciplined: Turn your smartphone in certain situations, such as when you are attending meetings, when you are driving, playing with your children or eating dinner with your family.

Ride the wave: When you get the overwhelming urge to check your phone. Relax, take a few mindful breaths and stay with the feeling rather than acting on it. This habit will gradually weaken your urge to check the phone every now and then.

Don't give up: If for some reason you relapse into your 24/7 phone/email checking habit, don't get discouraged and feel defeated. Try again.

Use your social media mindfully

Today social media such as LinkedIn, Twitter and Facebook are part of life. Often companies invest a large amount of assent to manage and promote their business through social media. Here are a few ways you can use social media mindfully:

View your business social media as a part of your working day. Therefore, when you are spending time with your family, turn it off. Use the business social media only during office hours.

Update your status at set times: Fix a time for social media. There are a lot of smart apps available to help you manage social media.

Be friendly: Don't see people as just another number or a status, behind each connection there is a human being. If they have an important question or comment, do respond.

Strive for honest connections rather than superficial contacts. Keep your contact list short.

Try to give more than you receive.

Chapter 16: Origins Of Mindfulness

Mindfulness meditation is something that is very beneficial for people because it relaxes them and allows them to have less stress in their lives. Since many people are taking to the mindfulness meditation, they are experiencing less stress and more joy in their lives. The reason is because this is a simple and easy type of meditation that calms peoples' nerves and allows them to be in control of many aspects of their lives that they wouldn't be able to do in other ways.

What Is Mindful Meditation?
Mindful meditation is something that people do in order to bring them to a calm state within their bodies and their minds. Mindfulness to an extent would have an effect on your mind just like vacationing would. They say taking a vacation here and there is good for you mind as it allows you to temporarily escape the stresses from the mundane world. This allows your brain

to recuperate to help you become more productive in the long run.

Mindfulness to a lesser degree does the same thing. It allows your mind to temporarily escape even if only for a few minutes, from the pressures of the mundane stressful world. This of course helps your brain to slightly recuperate which can help you deal with stress, depression and other mental issues or dilemmas one may have in life.

Since it takes a little practice to shut out the rest of the stressful world and all its responsibilities, it might take a little bit of time for people to be able to do this on a regular basis. Once they get used to practicing it however, they will find the benefits to be astounding.

They will feel less stressful in their lives, and they will be able to handle their responsibilities in a better manner. Due to the nature of our ultra-competitive world and the stress and hardships that often times come with it, people will love the benefits that practicing this type of meditation will do for them and how it can help them deal with today's crazy stressful environment.

Where Did Mindful Meditation Originate From?

The art of mindful meditation is from the Buddhist background. The Buddhists wanted to find a way to push hatred, delusion and greed from their minds. They used the mindful mediation to get to that point where it doesn't exist anymore. It is known that the Buddhists used mindfulness as a way to reach wisdom and enlightenment. Today psychologists have adopted the practice of mindfulness to help patients with many ailing conditions such as depression and anxiety.

Practicing mindfulness requires people to be of a determined and mindful frame of mind. They need to be able to put everything else out of their mind in order to concentrate on what is happening in that moment. They don't advise to do it too much at the beginning of practicing it because it can lead to being lazy. Once they are accustomed to the practice, they can then do so as often as they see fit.

Chapter 17: How To Listen Mindfully

A distinct difference exists between hearing someone and truly listening to them. By the traditional definition, hearing means taking in information or sound using your ears. But listening means focusing in on sound or giving your focus to something or someone, with the intention of understanding. When you truly listen to a person you take the time to hear them. However, when you just hear an event or person, you aren't necessarily truly listening. Traditional concepts and definitions are one thing, but let's take some time to consider the difference between hearing and listening.

How does Listening differ from Simply Hearing?

To fully listen means to give your complete attention to whoever you are talking to. This means staying present with a person to hear what their words are meaning to get across, including their emotions and words. Listening means you are hearing using all of you, and not just your ears. Consider an instance where you were conversing with a therapist, spouse, or friend about something important going on, and you left the discussion feeling cared about, loved, and all around lighter than you did entering it. This is what happens when someone truly listens to you, which is harder than it may sound on the surface. Hearing something does not mean truly taking it in.

Why doesn't everyone Listen?

Given these descriptions, it may seem obvious that everyone should listen, but to do this for real takes work and mindfulness. This requires giving your attention completely, and most of us have been trained to prioritize multi-tasking.

The Norm of Splitting your Attention: This means making food as you help your children do their school work, or exercising while you watch a movie. It's hard to give our full attention to just one activity as we do it, especially given our busy schedules that make this even more difficult. Many times, when we are in the mode of listening, we are also thinking of all of the tasks waiting for us that we must remember to get to, meaning we are not present for the talk as it happens.

To Truly Listen: When you are really listening to a person who is talking, you are giving them space and permission to express their truest feelings and thoughts. You are inviting them to share with you and helping them feel at peace, comfortable, and welcomed. When someone is truly listened to, they know they are in a loving situation and caring hands.

Some people find true listening to be effortless and natural, but for most of us, this is a skill that needs to be constantly worked on and practiced often. Think about it as a muscle that must be worked on to become stronger. It's hard to use it at first, but this grows easier with time and eventually becomes simple.

Using True Listening as a Meditative Practice:

The essence of meditation is focusing our minds with intention. This practice trains our emotions, thoughts, body, and mind to be present and still, accepting anything that happens, and takes plenty of practice. Similar to the practice of sitting meditation, listening as a meditative practice means staying still with whatever the other person says. This relies on conscious intention to keep your attention on something specific.

Actionable Steps for Making Listening a Practice of Mindfulness:

Next time you find yourself with an opportunity to listen to another person, think of it as a meditative practice. Think about not just receiving the input they are giving you, but listening with your entire being. Use these following steps to do so.

Focus: Pay full attention to whoever is talking to you, freeing yourself from any distractions that may pop up. This means silencing your cell phone and notifications, turning off the TV, and going to a quiet place. When your mind tries to stray from the conversation, gently bring it back to focus on your conversation partner. Similar to a meditation session, remind yourself to stay focused.

Stay in the Now: This is the perfect time to practice real present-ness. No one enjoys speaking with someone and having to repeat what they just said because the other was not listening. Prevent this by being entirely present and casting away your worries about the future, past, or other irrelevant information that is not related to the talk at hand.

Be Welcoming: Part of this practice will be welcoming whatever happens to appear at that moment. This should happen regardless of whether you disagree with the person or completely agree with them.

Invite the feelings and thoughts that the person is exploring, and allow them space to review them. This doesn't mean validating everything they say, but only being there to support them as a listener.

Hold back Reactions: Try keeping your body language and expressions warm and neutral, without reacting strongly to their words. You may find yourself wishing to react to what they say, but hold back and simply listen and be present. Your chance to share your opinions, stories, and advice will come, but now is not the time. This will take a lot of patience, especially if you aren't used to doing this.

Practice Understanding: This is a great opportunity to learn something by taking in what they are saying and attempting to really understand it. This step requires that you follow the steps listed above. Being unfocused means that you are more likely to misunderstand or entirely miss part of what they are saying. This makes it more likely that who you're talking to will feel as though they were not really heard. When you actually listen, the other person is much more likely to ask you what your thoughts are, and return the favor.

Practicing this will give you ample chances to learn about others, bringing you and the person you are conversing with to a stronger bond. This is why we converse with each other anyway, to feel connected. Why bother engaging in a talk if you aren't bothering to listen? Doing this will transform your life and bring you deeper connections.

Chapter 18: Who You Really Are

You are an expression of life itself. If you see reality as it is, you are life, just as trees, flowers, animals, and the earth are expressions of life itself, so are you. Your mind creates a concept called 'my life', but really to think that's who you are is to limit yourself in the most extreme way. It's like seeing a chrysalis and saying who you are is the cocoon and missing the magnificence of what's inside. You are not just the shell. You do not experience a life, you are life. You have an intelligence within, that makes your heart beat, that keeps you breathing, that makes every cell in your body operate.

At some level, you have always existed. Matter cannot be created or destroyed. You are energy, life force. The physical form changes, transforms, but you cannot disappear. Your mind-identified self fights for survival, fears annihilation, but the truth is, you do not die. Nothing can ever destroy you.

Nothing has an ego. Plants, animals, flowers, rocks, trees, the moon, dirt, the sea have no ego. Even human beings have no ego. We are responding to something that's not really there. It's an imaginary identity we acquire, like actors on a stage. It's like you're watching a movie and interacting with a character on the movie screen. The person on the movie screen isn't really there. We act like it's real, but at the deepest level, it is not there.

When you are interacting with others, look beyond the imagined self-identity the person has created. It's not who they really are. It's a persona, an actor, a character they have created. The ego causes separation, but it's made up. It's an illusion and we're living like it's real. When we begin to see things clearly, we can see beyond the antics, beyond the noise and we realize that everything is sacred. When there is no ego, you have reverence for everybody and everything.

Getting to the source of who you really are, or self-realization is attained by discovering what you are not. You can never know by trying to find out what it is.

The real self is not your body, it is not your mind, it is not your thoughts, it is not your beliefs, it is not your personality, it is not your opinions. It is not any of those things. All of these things are either always changing and things you've acquired. Anything you acquire cannot be you. When you've gone through everything and there's nothing left, that's what it is. Nothing. Emptiness. Now, with that clean slate, with the emptiness as a starting point, you can engage in the world with a sense of ease and freedom, a playfulness, knowing that the real self is untouchable.

The real you can't be destroyed by the actions of others. Go deep and reconnect with the deepest part of you, the part that has just observed the pain. The part that remains strong and peaceful no matter what.

Why are you afraid? What can the world do to you? Nothing.

You can engage with the material world, with ideas, but you're not attached to them or identified with them. You are free.

Distraction

Almost everyone I've ever worked with reports feeling a sense of loneliness, emptiness, or unfulfillment that they just can't shake. Some have described it as a hollow feeling, a void, or an empty feeling. This issue must be addressed from existential perspective.

You may look around and think most people seem okay. This is because they create a surface-level happiness, a facade that masks their true pain. As previously mentioned, people attempt to avoid the emptiness inside by creating distractions.

We've developed socially acceptable ways of escaping reality. Watching television, social media, incessant use of phones, having sex, making money, getting in and out of relationships, overworking, shopping, watching sports, drinking, using drugs…all are ways in which people attempt to avoid stillness. They need to avoid stillness because the pain and emptiness is always there, just underneath the distraction.

As long as the distraction is there, they feel 'okay', but never really truly happy or at ease. They jump from one distraction to the next, the next degree, accomplishment, material possession, relationship, etc. You can never get enough of what you don't need. You get temporary relief but the emptiness is always there.

Thoughts can be used to create specific life situations that appear satisfying on the surface level. These things have no existential relevance, only psychological or social relevance. Caring about what others think of you has no existential relevance.

Stop trying to control your mind

If you are very identified with your mind, with your thoughts, you won't be able to quiet your mind. If you are identified with your body, your looks, your clothes, your age, your politics, your status, your money, your title, you will constantly worry about losing these things or becoming more thought these things, trying to enhance your sense of self through these things.

Try to create a little distance from the mind. Even if it's a noisy mind, it's still okay. Just notice the noise, disengage from identifying with all the thoughts.

You do this by bringing your full attention to the present moment. Noticing, being aware of what's actually happening now instead of thinking about future or past.

Once you disengage from the mind, you disengage from all identity, because the mind is the one who creates all the identities. Identity exists in past or future, but not in the now. Your identity is either what you know about yourself regarding past experiences or what you think you will become in the future. Your 'identity' doesn't exist in the now.

Where is the self that you refer to? If all your attention is here, there is no self. The 'self' dissolves and all that's left is pure awareness, true freedom. We want to look good in other people's eyes, we want to belong. We become concerned with consumerism in an effort to fit in. We aspire to be good enough. We are less connected with others. We engage in less meaningful interactions. "Making it" or "having it all" is not the answer. Think of the celebrities who have it all and are so unhappy they are plagued with addictions. Some find life so unbearable it brings them to the point of suicide. We need to re-humanize our lives. We need to shift from competition and comparison to cooperation and connection.

Becoming fully involved in life

When you no longer depend on the world to make you happy, you are able to become fully involved in life without fear of losing yourself when things don't go your way. Be fully involved, but not dependent on your relationships, your job, you looks, your material things to make you happy. Fear of getting attached leads to avoidance of life. You can't fully experience life if you're not involved.

Be involved fully in every aspect of life, even the simplest acts, and life will be extraordinary. Your perceptions become distorted when you become identified with something or someone. For example, when you become identified, defined by, your romantic relationship, it feels as if you'll die if they leave you. In reality, your life does not depend on this person choosing to be with you, but your perceptions are so distorted because you identify your 'self' with the relationship.

Don't create an identity out of anything outside of yourself. Stay rooted in your being, knowing you are whole and complete, then fully engage in the world.

Externally derived happiness

If you depend on external things and circumstances to make you happy, you will suffer. What brings you happiness today will bring you suffering tomorrow. It's okay to enjoy things, but if you do those things or have those relationships in order to be happy, that will lead to pain. If you become attached to those people or things for a sense of happiness, then you are at risk of crumbling when those things or relationships no longer exist. Find the happiness within before you engage in worldly pursuits. That way you can fully enjoy those people and things without the fear of the inevitable loss. Most people can't enjoy pleasant things once they obtain them because they are always afraid they will lose them. Become fully involved in life but don't derive your sense of self-worth or happiness from that involvement.

Everything emanates from your mind

Nothing that you experience ever happens outside of yourself. Everything that happens to you, happens within you. You can't experience anything 'out there'. It always happens 'in here'. Your perception shapes your reality. If you reflect on every experience you've ever had, what you saw, felt, thought, heard, perceived, it was always experienced from within you.

The realization that everything that appears is a manifestation of your mind is your liberation, because that means you have control over how you respond to your own experiences. Nothing outside of you is in your control. Only what is inside of you is in your control. This leads to another very important point: stop trying to control things outside of you.

Everything is fleeting

Life as we live it in human form is fleeting. Nothing lasts. We have expectations that things will last forever, like relationships, jobs, roles, titles, material things. None of these things will last forever. Loss is a part of life. Change is constantly happening. You will eventually lose everyone that you love, either through physical death, or the relationship will come to an end or the nature of the relationship will change (such as when children grow up and leave the home).

This realization allows us to fully appreciate our loved ones when they're in our presence because we understand that they won't always be there. When you're enjoying coffee with your partner, you'll be there fully, soaking in the moment, knowing one day he or she won't be there. When you're working, you'll understand that you won't always work there. When you're with your children you'll know that they will grow up and leave. When you're with your parents, you'll know they'll grow old and die. When you're engaged in physical activity, you'll recognize that one day, if you live long enough, you will get sick. You will lose your physical abilities. Everyone will die. You will die. There is no right age for someone to die. If you love that person, it will never feel like the right time.

Content vs. Context

Content versus context essentially refers to doing versus being. Many people find themselves doing all the 'right' things, but never really feeling happy or fulfilled. It's like they're going through the motions and still, things don't work out. "But I did what I was supposed to do!"

For example, you can read books and learn things about how to make relationships work, so you can get the content right, but if the context in which you take those actions is "I'm unlovable", "I'm unworthy" "I'm not good enough", it won't matter what you do. It still won't work. Information (content) is actually a small part of the equation compared to who you're being (context).

Who you're being, what you believe, the filter from which you live your life determines the outcome. Many of us focus on learning more, learning skills and going through the motions. If the context isn't addressed, it doesn't matter what you do or how much you know. You will always feel that something is lacking, a void, emptiness, unfulfilled, lonely. I can't stress this enough: until you get the context right, it won't matter what you do (content).

Shifting the context means focusing more on the human being instead of the human doing.

Chapter 19: Advanced Tips For Relieving Workplace Stress

With the five minute program we just went over, you should be able to cope with most stressors that you encounter. However, some situations present additional challenges that require more advanced means of being mindful. With that in mind, I've put together a group of quick tips that you can review and practice to deal with any challenging circumstance.

We'll first start with old advice. A problem shared is a problem halved. Not long ago, academics at USC's Marshall School of Business tested this idea and found that there was a strong correlation with collaborative efforts and reduced stress. Taking the time to work through a problem with a colleague will enable you to approach the problem with an improved outlook and less stress.

Interestingly, this often seems at odds with our experience. When I am facing a tight deadline, my instinct is to just lower my head and push to complete the work. What USC's study suggests is that in those moments, a quick conversation or discussion with another stakeholder will help me work more effectively.

On a more basic level, talking with a friend or co-worker about anything, even non-work related topics, can have that same effect of diminishing stress. So simply connecting with the person one desk over for a few minutes of idle conversation can help. If you apply a healthy dose of mindfulness to either of these techniques, you will be more aware in the moment of how the conversation is providing a sense of calm confidence necessary for your long term success.

The next piece of advice I want to offer is similarly commonsensical. Though like many articles of common sense, we tend to ignore its usefulness. One can prevent and alleviate stress by practicing consistent self-care. Whenever we delay taking care of our basic needs to finish our work, we are amplifying the stress we feel. I have been very guilty of this. I'll have a project I need to wrap up and though my stomach is growling and I feel very hungry, I will postpone taking lunch until I'm done.Hunger just amplifies the stress I feel and makes it more difficult for me to finish my project. That's true no matter what I do to neglect my own physical needs. When I stay up too late to finish an assignment, not only does my work suffer, I physically suffer from exhaustion.

When you feel hunger, stop what you are doing and focus on your body and how it feels. If you need food, eat. If you need water, get it. If you need to take a break to clear your mind, do it. If you need to stop for the night and rest, sleep. Your body is unambiguous about what it needs. We try to postpone self-care in the interests of finishing our work. This only harms us. As you practice more mindful self-care your stress will decrease, your work will improve and you will feel a greater sense of peace and calm.

As we alluded to in Chapter 3, physical exercise can have a positive benefit on stress. This is also an aspect of healthy self-care. Sitting at our desks, staring at illuminated screens, under the glare of fluorescent bulbs, we absorb so much environmental stress. Our bodies are not meant to do this kind of work for extended periods of time.

The best cure is to build time into your day to go to the gym. Even if it's a quick run on a treadmill or a little time on the rowing machine, the physical activity releases chemicals that reduce stress in our bodies and minds. We feel lighter and stronger and more confident for the balance of our workday.

As you practice body scans and other meditative techniques, apply those to your workouts. You'll literally feel the strength building in your arms, legs and core as you work out, which will only serve to motivate you to work out more.

Finally, let go of mistakes. We all fail from time to time. I get stressed just like everyone else. Sometimes I can cope and soothe myself effectively. Other times the stress controls me. When that happens, I used to beat myself up and heap on more stress because I was such a failure.

Among the most important measures of mindfulness is to accept yourself as you are. Every one of us makes mistakes and fails from time to time. Being mindful of our imperfections and accepting them as part of who we are allows us to cope with the things we don't like about ourselves, even while we strive to fix them.

So let's go back to our list of stressors we made in the beginning. Think about the one you underlined and all the exercises we have discussed. Which exercises and techniques will lend themselves best to addressing your major source of stress?

Write those down next to it. Then go through the rest of the list and note which exercises will help.

This week, I want you to apply those exercises to the stressful situations you encounter at work and measure how well they help. This is also a mindfulness exercise. In doing so you will train your mind to accept stress, to feel it in the moment and to release it.

Chapter 20: Stress And Flow States

We're only halfway through the book and already you should have picked up some pretty useful skills. You now know how to enter a mindful state at any given time to better appreciate your surroundings or at least just to escape stress for a few moments of respite.

But let's rewind and look at that stress in a little more detail. What is it about stress that makes it so serious? Why are we trying to combat stress? And is stress **always** bad?

Actually, stress is something that is sorely misunderstood by a lot of people. Stress is not really 'one thing', rather it is a spectrum of responses that occur in response to dangerous situations. Essentially, when you detect danger, your body response by releasing hormones and neurotransmitters that trigger the 'fight or flight' response. This is the response that we described earlier and it is modulated by the following hormones/neurotransmitters (neurotransmitters are like hormones but they affect the brain more directly and don't last as long):

Dopamine

Epinephrine

Norepinephrine

Serotonin

Cortisol

Glutamate

Testosterone

Oestrogen

These then together cause a number of symptoms that you should be familiar with if ever you've gotten into an argument, fight or dangerous predicament. And if you haven't… who are you??

These symptoms include:

Sense of dread

Racing thoughts

Shaking

Muscle contractions

Vasodilation (widening of the veins)

Increased heartrate

Pupil dilation

Resistance to pain

Suppression of the immune system and digestive system so that more blood and resources can be sent to the brain and muscles

Increased sensitivity to sounds and light

Tunnel vision

Rapid breathing

Sweating

Increased blood viscosity to encourage the blood to clot in case of an injury

In short, our body goes into a 'high performance mode' by diverting energy and supplies away from maintenance tasks and less immediately urgent processes. Our strength, speed and ability to fight or climb increase and this makes us more powerful and better able to respond.

This response evolved in the wild in order to help us protect ourselves in case of danger. If we saw a predator, or if we saw a forest fire, then these changes would help us escape. Likewise, we would become better fighters when competing with members of our own species for resources.

And sometimes in the modern world, this response can be exactly what we need. If a mugger pulls a knife on you, then this will give you the best chance of running away to live another day.

Chronic Stress

But the problem comes when the threat isn't a physical threat and when it isn't an 'immediate' threat. We simply live in a world that we didn't evolve for and this means that many of our systems are essentially outdated.

For example, if you're giving a speech, then your body will react in just the same way as it would if you saw a forest fire. And in this case, none of the changes would help at all. You'd be more likely to stutter, you'd look sweaty and your voice might even change.

And if you panic (sometimes stress can feel like a heart problem!) then this can eventually create a vicious circle causing you to get more and more stressed – eventually hyperventilating and passing out as a result. This is what happens in the case of an anxiety attack!

Moreover, this is also how we respond to being in debt. Or hating our jobs. Or waiting to hear back about an offer we put on a house.

But we can't run away from these problems and we can't fight them. And this then means that the fight or flight response can continue on a 'low level' for a long duration of time. This is what we call chronic stress and it's bad for all **kinds** of reasons.

For starters, chronic stress means that our immune system and digestion are suppressed for long periods of time. This can lead to malabsorption as we become less able to extra nutrients from our food.

And it can prevent us from sleeping and make us more immune to disease.

What's more, is that eventually this stress can cause us to 'run out' of the catecholamine neurotransmitters that allow us to focus. This is called 'adrenal fatigue' and it's linked with depression and chronic anxiety.

Note as well that no neurotransmitter and no hormones work in a vacuum. If you increase one, you alter others. And when you increase cortisol (associated with chronic stress in particular) you also increase ghrelin – the hunger hormone. This also encourages something called 'lipogenesis' meaning that more of the fuels in your diet will be stored as fat rather than used for energy. In fact, cortisol even breaks down muscle by producing something called myostatin which signals the body to break down muscle for energy. So it's important for your physique as well that you learn not to feel stressed when it isn't useful.

This is why it's so important that we learn to respond appropriate to the situation at hand and to suppress stress when it isn't appropriate – so that we can carry on enjoying life and staying healthy.

Mindfulness is the path to that eventuality.

Positive Stress

But the thing is, there is such thing as 'positive stress'. The aim here is not to completely remove stress from your life, rather it is just to control it.

As we've already seen, stress is a positive tool if you're trying to enhance your physical performance. If you're in a race, or if you're surfing, then this response is exactly what you need in order to get things done.

But the ideal situation would be that you get all the benefits of the fight or flight response, without the negatives. Imagine if you could gain that focus and that increased muscle mass but **without** the sense of dread and fear.

As it happens, just such a state may exist. This is what psychologists call a 'flow state' and it tends to be triggered during moments where we are highly focussed on something that we also actually enjoy. The example given most often is extreme spots, where some athletes describe the world seeming to slow down around them while they pull off amazing moves and feel more alive than they ever have done.

We also experience flow when we're completely focussed on the work we're doing, or when we're so deep in concentration that we forget the time and speak through the night. During this state, we product similar neurotransmitters and hormones but with the addition of another one called 'anandamide' – the bliss hormone that is also connected to abstract and creative thinking. It's actually the same chemical that gives marijuana its effect but what most people don't know is that it's also produced naturally by the brain.

Remember though that again this isn't really just 'one state' but rather a spectrum. We can be slightly stressed and very stressed. We can be slightly alert, or very alert. We can be alert and angry, alert and happy or alert and scared. It's useful to think of the brain in terms of 'states' but just be aware that there are countless states **in between** as well and it's more likely that you're somewhere here on the spectrum.

Flow states help us to perform at our best and focus more but they don't cause the same negative effects as a typical fight or flight. The difference? Enjoyment. So if you can try and tap into the enjoyment of what you're doing and see it as a fun **challenge** rather than something terrible, then you're more likely to get into that flow. Find the fun in what you're doing, find what you're passionate about in it and learn to actually enjoy it. You can do all this using very similar strategies to the cognitive restructuring we've already seen.

And likewise, you also need a low level of 'eustress'. Eustress is the equivalent of chronic stress but is once again a more positive form. Eustress is the kind of stress that motivates us to do things. For example, if you have an exam coming up and you don't experience any stress at all, then there is a good chance that you're not going to revise for it and as such, you won't get very good grades. Having just the right amount of low level 'stress' is what you need to make sure you start revising early and do the best you can. Eustress doesn't just have to mean negative motivation, it can also mean positive motivation – for instance stress that you might not achieve the things you really want to achieve. It's stress but it's based around something positive.

Tapping Into Hidden Powers

Then there's the type of stress that can unlock even more physical and mental potential. I'm not saying that anyone is going to be able to train themselves to the point where they can access this potential; all I'm saying is that it exists which is highly interesting and hopefully outlines the possibilities that exist and the reason that accessing more of your mind and your emotions is so potentially powerful.

So with that in mind, the first example is something called a 'flashbulb memory'. This demonstrates the ability we have to memorize things in vivid detail if we think the event is important enough. Think back to where you were at the time you first heard of the 9/11 attacks, or perhaps where you were when you first heard about Michael Jackson. Alternatively, consider a moment that was particularly important in your own life – for good or for bad.

Conclusion

Mindfulness is an attitude that requires you to first slow down in your life so that you become faster and more productive later on. While it may seem to be counterproductive to slow down, you will notice that after a few days of consciously slowing down and doing things mindfully will make you far more productive than if you tried to multitask or do things fast and mindlessly.

You need to stop and rest before becoming strong enough to handle your life better. Let me illustrate this through a simple example. Suppose you work 24/7 without any sleep. How would it be? I am sure many of you have experienced this for a short time when preparing for an exam or an important project. The experience of working without rest is very, very unpleasant. Rest, undoubtedly, increases efficiency and effectiveness.

It is, therefore, essential to stop your mindless running helter-skelter for some time, get a new perspective in your life, find meaning in it, and then work again at achieving your desires in a more effective and efficient way than before. Stopping to become mindful of your life and the activities in it is a way of stopping or slowing down so that you can get a better quality life than before. Living a life of practiced mindfulness is the way to that joyous conclusion.

The best way of becoming mindful is by allowing your mind to go wherever it wants to. Let it go from thought to thought while you simply sit back and watch and observe how the mind is moving. Being mindful does not mean controlling the mind. In fact, controlling the mind has an effect that is the exact opposite of mindfulness. The mind will move around, but its natural ability is that it finds its ways back to the present. It is this natural ability that you need to leverage to practice mindfulness.

When the mind comes back after it riotous route of traveling all over, it will be calm and still because it understands that there is no bliss like the present moment. When you realize the power of being in the present, you will find peace and happiness and anxiety and stress will go straight out of the window.

I hope the tips, advice, and suggestions in this book have motivated you to start looking at leading your life more mindfully so that you can all the benefits of this amazing way of life.

Finally, I would like to tell you that no matter which method you choose to take up, practice is the key element in learning and mastering the art of mindfulness. Use the art of mindfulness and read every chapter in this book again going through and understanding them little by little. Take each kind of attitude explained to you one at a time and diligently put it to

Belongs instead of unloading it onto your children and passing it along to the next generation, and of renewal to open the pathway to a more peaceful and gentle approach to parenting.

Preview...
• Introduction to the basics
• Understand the causes behind child aggressive behavior
• How to spot the signs of anger in toddlers
• Is my kid an angry toddler? The test you should take
• How you should interpret the anger test
• Coping mechanisms for mom's & dad's
• How kids can learn anger management
• Strategies to help your angry toddler channel their aggression
• How to improve the bond between you & you kid
• How to bring happiness back into your home
• And much more...

You will learn how to let go of frustration and prevent fighting, arguing, and resistance. The end result will be a peaceful and constructive relationship with a well-behaved child who feels appreciated and loved.

use in your life. Be mindful of that particular attitude. Then, move on to the next and become mindful of that and so forth. With practice, patience, and diligence you will reap the benefits of mindful living sooner than later.

www.ingramcontent.com/pod-product-compliance
Lightning Source LLC
Chambersburg PA
CBHW072009070526
44583CB00015B/1406